AFRICA

THE PRIMACY OF
POLITICS

STUDIES IN POLITICAL SCIENCE

AFRICA
THE PRIMACY OF
POLITICS

HERBERT J. SPIRO
Editor

EDOUARD BUSTIN

BOSTON UNIVERSITY

HENRY BRETTON

UNIVERSITY OF MICHIGAN

CLEMENT HENRY MOORE

UNIVERSITY OF CALIFORNIA AT BERKELEY

THOMAS HOVET, JR.

NEW YORK UNIVERSITY

HERBERT J. SPIRO

UNIVERSITY OF PENNSYLVANIA

Random House ❧ *New York*

PREFACE

The simplest test of quality I know for books on African politics asks whether the analysis still makes sense by the time of publication. Many books fail this test, either because their authors get so entangled in the undergrowth of petty facts that they lose sight of any pattern that may be emerging in their particular jungle, or because they reason by false analogy to the (occasionally misunderstood or misinterpreted) politics of other areas of the world in other eras of its history.

As editor of this little book, and as the convener of the panel of scholars who wrote it, I am happy that it passes my test, more than two years after our original meeting. No reasonable and knowledgeable student of politics in Africa would claim "timelessness" for his work. The best we can expect is that we contribute toward the collection of data and the refinement of methods. The co-authors of this book, having added to the body of known facts elsewhere, are here more interested in the second task.

Except for the editor's contributions, all chapters were prepared for the annual meeting of the African Studies Association, held in San Francisco, in October 1963. In addition to these four contributions, the Political Science Panel also enjoyed the comments of Professor John H. Kautsky of Washington University (St. Louis) which he preferred not to have included in the book.

Since my four colleagues dealt with different geographical, substantive, and methodological problem areas, their chapters contain little mutual give-and-take. I saw it as the editor's function to make up for this unavoidable defect. The other contributors have read neither my *Introduction*, nor the chapter on *The Primacy of Political Development*. As a result, there may be more editorial "give" than "take," for which I gladly assume full responsibility. The sovereign in the modern state has been described by political science as that authority which has the last word. As editor of this Study in Political Science I find myself in an analogous but superior position to the sovereign, because I have both the last word and the first.

Herbert J. Spiro

Philadelphia
November, 1965

CONTENTS

AFRICA

THE PRIMACY OF
POLITICS

INTRODUCTION

There was a distinct shortage of literature on politics in Africa until roughly 1960. Since then, however, the American reading public has been deluged with books, many of them paperbacks, about general and particular aspects of political Africa. Some of the books espouse particular causes, some make current events more conveniently accessible, others lay the foundations for scholarly analysis of rapid and radical changes, the flood of which seems even more overwhelming than that of the literature itself.

The quality of scholarly efforts to digest this floodtide has varied greatly. This was to be expected of analyses of an area in which Westerners not working for one of the European colonial powers had little previous interest or preparation. Most recent work by American social scientists has been stimulated by generous foundation crash programs designed to remedy this situation. Fellowships and travel grants made it possible for established scholars to apply their conventional tools to African phenomena (and in some cases to refashion these tools), and for aspirant members of the relevant professions to learn their disciplines and develop their skills within an African context.

Students of politics have responded to their confrontation with Africa with widely differing attitudes. At one extreme are those who assert that there is nothing new under the sun—not even the African sun. Human nature is always and everywhere the same and, therefore, human

responses to similar problems are going to be similar. If
African countries today are facing the same problems that
Latin American countries faced in the last century, and
that Southeast Asian lands faced in the last twenty years,
then African politics will resemble Latin American or
Southeast Asian politics of these parallel periods. There
will be Balkanization, corruption, and violence; deep
gulfs between rulers and ruled; great dangers of Communist subversion and take-overs.

At the other extreme we hear radical assertions of the
novelty and uniqueness of "Black Africa" and its politics.
This part of the world achieved independence and statehood in peculiarly auspicious circumstances, with a minimum of organized violence (prior to 1961), with aid
from the United Nations and from lessons drawn from the
less happy experience of those very regions whose history
the opposite persuasion sees being repeated in Africa. If
political development and economic, social, and cultural
modernization can be brought to Africa from wherever
their highest forms have been achieved, then Africa will
be able to "skip stages" in its evolution. Conventional
nationalism has not yet evolved and, if it fails to do so,
prospects are brighter for African unification than for
Latin American or European unification. In view of this
purported uniqueness, African institutions and practices
must not be judged by simple comparison with their
apparent counterparts elsewhere. There are, for example,
African One-Party States, according to the title of a book
edited by Professor Gwendolen M. Carter, that are quite
different from one-party systems in Eastern Europe, the
southern United States, or Latin America.

Although only a few scholars have taken one of these
two extreme stands in interpreting African politics—and
heated debates have been generated between them—most
interpretations fall closer to the midpoint between the

poles: Human nature is indeed the same everywhere and at all historically known times (these students seem to be saying), but in some cases the conditions under which the new African states emerged into independence and world politics were in fact different, and some of the results consequently unprecedented. We should, nevertheless, evaluate these results by reference to the same standards of judgment that are, according to these middle-of-the-roaders, universally valid. For example, corruption is corruption, whether it occurs in Nicaragua or Nigeria; preventive detention is a tool of the police state, whether it is practiced in Aachen or Accra.

Controversy in a field of study is generally a sign of youth and vigor, so we should welcome these character-istics of recent American writings on African politics. But if we also expect controversy to yield a clearer definition of the issues, then we should be disappointed with the current state and direction of political "African studies." In few instances have the issues under debate, and the problems for further study and thought, been clearly delineated. Dissatisfaction with this state of affairs first prompted me to propose "The Primacy of Politics in Africa" as the topic of the political science panel I had been asked to organize for the Sixth Annual Meeting of the African Studies Association, held in San Francisco on October 25, 1963.

I posed this topic as a series of questions to the distinguished political scientists on the panel: Is politics primary in Africa? That is, are political considerations accorded greater importance than economic, social, cul-tural, and other nonpolitical considerations, both inside Africa and in Africa's relations with the rest of the world? Does this primacy of politics stand up to compari-sons between Africa and other areas? How can we prove or disprove that it makes sense to speak of the primacy of politics in Africa? In either case, what consequences for further research and thought, and for policy, can we draw from this statement of the issue and—possibly—from any conclusions upon which we may agree?

I was, of course, not the first to ask the question about the primacy of politics in Africa. It has provided a background for many discussions ever since Kwame Nkrumah exhorted his followers (including those outside the Gold Coast) to seek first the political kingdom, for all else would be added unto them once it—that is, self-government and independence—had been won. Under Nkrumah's leadership, his approach "worked." Although his opponents asserted that the colony was not ready for independence—economically, socially, and otherwise— independence was gained very quickly; and subsequently, much greater advances were made in remedying the nonpolitical shortcomings than had been made under colonialism. Pragmatically speaking, Nkrumah proved himself right in proposing the sequence of politics first, then everything else. The Belgians, whose policy in the Congo was based on the reverse sequence—no politics until after achievement of economic and educational advances—were proved wrong by events in the Congo after June 1960.

All the independence movements in Africa, whether or not they adopted Nkrumah's motto explicitly, used it as a basis for action. All opponents of the independence movements rejected its validity. The Portuguese, for example, did so on grounds of principle; for a time they insisted on considering their colonies integral provinces of the metropole and therefore refused even to countenance the possibility of a separate political existence for Angola, Mozambique, and Portuguese Guinea. Others merely opposed the speed with which African colonies sought to stand on their own feet despite, *inter alia,* their lack of economic "viability." Regardless of the rationale for or the degree of opposition to independence, the argument always ended by telling the Africans that other things were more important than full participation in politics and self-government. Your country lacks the "prerequisites" for "stable democracy."[1] You should try to "make up" these prerequisites before you wholly throw off White control of your government.

Since those who rejected these arguments won out, and since the largest bloc of new members admitted to the United Nations has been from Africa, the same debate has been repeated in and about the United Nations. The older, predominantly White and Western member states complain about the inexperience and alleged irresponsibility of the new African members. They object to the principle of "one state—one vote," operative in the General Assembly, just as opponents of self-government in Africa objected to the slogan, "one man—one vote." In their colonies, the Western nations could for a time introduce complicated voting systems designed to relate the franchise to economic and educational requirements. Some seem to wish they could alter the voting system of the General Assembly to base its franchise at least upon ability to pay, and at most upon ability to shoot—that is, relative "power." Even the Soviet Union seems occasionally to be dismayed by African participation in debates on nuclear arms control and disarmament.

African leaders, however, at home and abroad, continue to act upon the assumption of the primacy of politics. In one sense it could be asserted that they are not really behaving differently from leaders anywhere else, that there are parallels between African conduct and the classical Western tradition whereby politics is the "master science." From this point of view one could say that

Westerners, as members of more mature and more highly
differentiated societies, simply distinguish among the
many different aspects of politics that take place below
and are coordinated by the politics of the state and of
political parties. In German, for example, a distinction is
made among *Staatspolitik, Parteipolitik, Wirtschaftspoli-
tik, Sozialpolitik,* and *Kulturpolitik.* The newly independent African countries are still relatively undifferentiated
in their social structures and in the functions performed
by their leaders. Hence they pour everything into the
single pot of politics. But once discernible, separate, and
self-conscious political, economic, social, and cultural
groups emerge within the elites (or to the extent that this
is already occurring), the basis for any discussion of the
primacy of politics in Africa will disappear.

With such considerations in mind, I approached the
other contributors to this little book. They came to the
topic from rather diverse backgrounds and fit into the
spectrum of attitudes described earlier at different points.
As a result, their articles approach the central question
from a variety of angles and on several levels of political
activity. The substantive materials for the first two articles were gathered in two countries, the Congo and
southern Nigeria. This does not mean, however, that
these papers are of interest only to readers who wish to
inform themselves about these two regions.

Professor Bustin addresses himself to the prevailing
Western bias about the Congo. This is not so much a bias
against the "Lumumbist" persuasion in Congolese politics
as it is a prejudice against Congolese politics *per se.*
Western analysts and policy-makers, with very few exceptions, have agreed that the Congo suffers from a plethora
of politics. Some view this simply as the local manifestation of a current African disease the symptoms of which
have been more visible in the Congo because of its

involvement in world politics and the consequent better coverage given it by both journalists and scholars. Most Western—and some non-Western—panaceas for the Congo have been based upon the same diagnosis: Get your economy back on an even keel; carry out a crash program of training for technicians and professional personnel; reorganize your army. This is what the Congo's leaders were told explicitly. Implicitly, it was suggested to them that the greatest service they could perform for their country would be to give up partisan politics and end the "hopeless squabbling" in parliament. Those who rendered this kind of advice in effect echoed the earlier Belgian denial of the primacy of politics. Professor Bustin examines this interpretation critically and rejects it.

Professor Bretton's survey of influence patterns in Southern Nigeria is of great interest for many reasons; I would select two for special attention. The first is his exhortation to begin empirical research on African politics of the kind that political scientists have been conducting for many years on the politics of other areas of the world. The time has passed, he asserts, when we can afford, or need, "to make generalizations based on generalizations derived from other generalizations." The second is the history of his own entry into the field of African studies. He first published an article on "Political Thought and Practice in Ghana" in March 1958, at a time when the first American political scientists specializing in Africa south of the Sahara were still generally uncritical of independence movements and of the government of Ghana, then the only newly independent state that had been a colony. He cautioned that

. . . the overly zealous application to underdeveloped areas of research methods derived from experience in advanced, highly developed countries leads to the promulgation of

wholly unrealistic theories. For instance, David Apter, for
some reason expecting parliamentary democracy to develop
in the Gold Coast, given certain conditions, bases upon this
expectation an elaborate theory of institutional transfer. His
utilization of advanced sociological principles to the Gold
Coast lends the experiment there—it is no more than that—
an unwarranted appearance of respectability and perma-
nence.[2]

Subsequently, in his *Power and Stability in Nigeria:
The Politics of Decolonization* (1962), Professor Bretton
again took a less sanguine, more critical view of the
prospects of the one new state in Africa about which even
Western opponents of President Nkrumah's regime had
been most optimistic. Turning to the focal question of our
book, Professor Bretton found that political considerations do indeed outweigh all other considerations. He
suggests, as a consequence of this primacy of politics, the
impossibility of rational economic planning or allocation
of resources. He also identifies the progressive fusion of
State, Party, and Society as a sign of an incipient totalitarian apparatus in Africa.

These suggestions illuminate a whole new facet of the
African political crystal. In the West—beginning with
Plato, according to some students—assertion of the primacy of politics occasionally led, both in logic and in fact,
to the extension of total politics, that is, to the establishment of totalitarianism. If it makes sense to speak of the
primacy of politics in Africa (regardless of the comparative uniqueness or conventionality of this phenomenon)
should we then also expect totalitarianism to follow? By
what sequence of stages will it develop, given such different starting points as those of the Congo (still suffering
from a dearth of politics, according to Professor Bustin),
and of Nigeria (where, according to Professor Bretton,

the Eastern Region under the monopolistic control of the National Council of Nigerian Citizens manifests the primacy symptoms in particular profusion) ?

Professor Moore seeks to isolate the distinctive features held in common by the party systems of the new African states and discusses the differences between these party systems and otherwise similar ones in Latin America, the Middle East, and elsewhere. He accepts Carl J. Friedrich's definition of totalitarianism and applies it in order to answer the question about incipient totalitarianism in Africa. The continental scope of his paper gives it special value. For, until recently, most political scientists studying Africa confined themselves to Africa south of the Sahara, leaving North Africa and the other predominantly Arab countries to our colleagues in Middle Eastern area studies. This self-restriction, which had obvious practical causes, involved certain disadvantages; African resentment at the alleged racial bias of this academically drawn boundary was not the least of them. Another handicap of this approach was the tendency, which it encouraged, to exaggerate the Sahara's role as a barrier when, in fact, it also served as a link for transport and communications along its "littoral."[3] Professor Moore finds it easy and reasonable to speak of the same type of party system on both, or all, sides of the boundary that our colleagues earlier thought it necessary or convenient to draw. Since his own field work was carried out mainly in Tunisia, his findings of such similarities may come as a surprise to some. But he derives his explanation from the "colonial dialectic" that all the African states now having mass party regimes lived through.

Professor Hovet's attitude toward African politics is in a way the most objective of those represented in this book, simply because he has been a student of politics, not in Africa, but in the United Nations. His study of

Bloc Politics in the United Nations (1960) was a pioneer-
ing effort in that it applied to the General Assembly a
method used previously to analyze voting behavior in
national parliaments. Because the African caucus in the
UN was the youngest and soon would become the largest
regional one, Professor Hovet subsequently took it as his
focus in *Africa in the United Nations* (1963). For the
purposes of that study, it did not matter whether the new
African states in their domestic politics were suffering
from a plethora or a dearth of politics. What mattered
was how they conducted themselves at the UN and
whether they were making optimum use of the opportunities that the international organization offered to Africa
as a whole.

Professor Hovet had studied African UN delegates and
gotten to know many of them on familiar terms, in the
environment of the United Nations and New York City.
He had never been to Africa, where the other contributors
to this book have done much of their work and, incidentally, formed similar personal acquaintanceships. But his
answer to the question about the primacy of politics is the
same: Africans at the UN do give a higher priority to
political considerations than do most delegates from other
regions. Moreover, and despite such handicaps as their
inexperience, they have taken readily to UN procedures,
skillfully exploiting them for the benefit of Africa (including its still dependent peoples), and have made some
creative procedural innovations for relations both among
themselves and with non-African members. Professor
Hovet also discusses the "responsibility" of African members of the United Nations.

Anyone who has studied the political behavior of Africans must notice—as all contributors to this book have
noticed—the extraordinary frankness with which most

Africans discuss matters that their counterparts on other continents usually classify as secret. At times African politicians are almost indiscreet in conversation with outsiders who, like ourselves, are studying their politics. This factor accounts for the rewarding acquaintances and indeed friendships that often result from professional contacts between social scientists and the objects of their study in Africa. This is one reason for the attractiveness of African politics as a special field of study—a reason that also contains some risks for the researcher's objectivity: He could easily "overidentify" with his friends in the country he is studying, or become unrealistically optimistic about "his" particular political system and, indeed, about Africa as an evolving political entity.

If these are possible consequences of African frankness, then the causes of this frankness are of equal interest. There are a number of different and related explanations of the comparative absence of a sense of secrecy in African politics: the lack of physical and social privacy in many African villages and towns, the absence of the European tradition of statehood with its notion of the *arcana imperii,* the populist qualities of the independence movements, the relative unimportance of the military, and the Africans' quite genuine naïveté about contemporary world affairs. But there is one more explanation derived from the essentially political outlook of the African elites. African leaders are keenly aware of the primacy of politics in and for their communities, though they may have no theoretical understanding of the foundations of this primacy. Moreover, they *like* politics, while in the Western and Eastern traditions, people either dislike politics or at best are ambivalent about it. And while administration, especially in the cameralist tradition, may thrive on secrecy, politics thrives on publicity: hence the Africans' frankness to the point of indiscretion and their

intellectual hospitality toward outside scholars who in-
quire into African politics.

The African notion of the primacy of politics manifests
itself in different ways, many of which are discussed in
the following articles. One rather unexpected—and possibly most beneficial—manifestation occurred in 1963, far
away from the bright African sun, during the gloomy
Russian winter. As earlier in Bulgaria, so now in the
Soviet Union, African students, principally from Ghana,
staged protest demonstrations. In Bulgaria, these demonstrations were set off by charges of racial discrimination;
in Russia, by the alleged killing of a Ghanaian student
about to marry a Russian girl. These events were widely
and rather gleefully reported by American news media,
because they were thought to prove that Soviet Commu-
nists, too, were guilty of discrimination, so that Africans
might become more tolerant of United States failings in
this respect.

This perspective of news analysis drew attention away
from what struck me as the most remarkable aspect of
these events: In the heart of the Soviet Union, literally at
the very gates of the ancient citadel of the Kremlin, a
small group of "foreign students," thousands of miles
away from their entirely different and comparatively
"primitive" homelands, were able spontaneously to organize an orderly public demonstration of political protest. High Soviet officials met and negotiated with representatives of the African students and apparently made
concessions to some of their demands. While it may be
unrealistic to expect Soviet citizens to learn anything
from this experience, it does illustrate dramatically and in
a novel context these Africans' political talents, among
them the capacities to organize, to deliberate issues, and
to commit themselves effectively to the resolution that has
been agreed upon. If they could bring these political

talents to bear upon their problems in the alien and unfavorable environment of the Soviet Union, their fellows at home and in world politics can perhaps be expected to make even more unconventional contributions to the growing global body of political practice.

1

THE QUEST FOR
POLITICAL STABILITY
IN THE CONGO:
SOLDIERS, BUREAUCRATS
AND POLITICIANS

EDOUARD BUSTIN

The importance ostensibly attached to economic development by virtually all newly independent states, whatever
their ideological coloring, as well as the prestige enjoyed
since Marx by economic determinism among Western (or
westernized) intellectual circles sometimes tends to obscure the importance of purely political problems for the
new states, especially those of Africa. Yet, in the attempt
to sort out ends and means, or to label causes and effects,
political and economic factors are often so thoroughly
entangled that terminological differentiations frequently
tend to become inane, if not misleading. Latter-day Marx-
ists themselves have long been aware of the fact that the
supposedly spontaneous operation of economic "rules"
could be altered by deliberate political action. As Lenin

put it bluntly during the controversy over the role of trade unions in January 1921: "Politics cannot but have precedence over economics; to argue otherwise is to forget the ABC of Marxism."[1] And, in a totally different context, an African echo answers with Kwame Nkrumah's well-known dictum: "Seek ye first the political kingdom . . . and all else shall be added unto it."

The validity of Nkrumah's words for Africa is supported by the increasingly accepted premise that economic development presupposes the existence of a polity where the organs of decision-making have crystallized to some extent, where the channels of power are set in a tolerably stable course (even though they may still remain uncharted), and where the articulation between political demands and the mobilization of popular support is sufficiently integrated into "frameworks of common, continuous political activity and organization, such as political parties."[2] Thus, to speak of the primacy of politics in Africa—or indeed in the world—may amount simply to a recognition of the fact that the preconditions of development and modernization are largely political, insofar as they involve a deliberate attempt to alter social patterns and attitudes in a given direction by a mixed recourse to persuasion and coercion.

To what extent have these political preconditions been met in Africa? The answer varies a great deal, of course, according to the specific case under consideration but, in general, it would seem that they have been met only in part. Furthermore, it is by no means certain that the social (let alone institutional) patterns of political power which have emerged in former colonial countries following their independence will remain unaltered for any substantial length of time, or evolve the capability of adjusting to new pressures and demands. The attainment of national independence answered a certain number of

political questions and clarified the quantities of a few
equations; but nowhere has it solved (except, perhaps, in
a very formal way through the medium of constitutional
instruments) the conflict between traditionality and
modernity or the problems posed by nation-building, by
the orderly transfer of power, and by popular participation in public life, nor has it stabilized the relationship
between the branches of the national government, or that
between governmental agencies and the single or dominant party.

The triangular relationship between the concepts of
nation, state, and *people,* which has been the fulcrum of
virtually all modern conceptions, misconceptions, and
vicissitudes regarding nationalism and democracy, has its
counterpart in Africa. Yet political change in Africa has
been unique in a number of respects, and notably in that,
in some cases at least (not only in the Congo), a state was
founded before national consciousness had completely
crystallized, or again, in that the formal trappings of
popular sovereignty were established before the political
socialization of the people had been achieved. Hence, one
notes the considerable importance attached to the institutional and juridical aspects of statehood (boundaries
being one of them, as well as membership in international
organizations) and even more, to the exercise of *imperium*—the right to employ the force of the state to
enforce the laws. There is also the considerable role
played in some new states by the major instruments of
state power: the armed forces and the bureaucracy. There
is indeed substantial evidence to suggest—at least as a
working hypothesis—that reliance on the normative and
coercive apparatus of the state tends to be maximized in
those countries where national consciousness and popular
mobilization are most deficient. In other words, where
political legitimacy is not unquestionably rooted in a

sufficiently widespread national sentiment or founded on a peremptory expression of popular will, it tends to be derived from such sources as control of the institutions, the effective use of state power, and adherence to a certain amount of legal formality.[3]

The redistribution of political power in colonial Africa took place in two stages, which the formal achievement of independence conveniently bisects for purposes of analysis, but does not really separate. The first stage is (or, increasingly, was) characterized by the forging of what has been called the "organizational weapon"[4] (in other words, the political party or coalition created for the purpose of wresting power from the colonial metropole). The second stage is marked by the simultaneous use of the party and of the state apparatus bequeathed by the colonial regime as power-controlling devices, with the emphasis being gradually placed upon the latter. Crudely speaking, one might say that whereas the problem used to be "how to get power," it is now "how to keep it" and "what to do with it"—or perhaps, more accurately, "what to do with it in order to keep it."[5] The answers to this last question have apparently been the determinant factors governing the allocation and delegation of power within most African states.

Among the many possible uses of power (notably political power), probably the two most obvious are the use of power as a self-regenerating agent (e.g., for the acquisition of additional power; the strengthening of social, economic, or electoral bases of support; the elimination of opposition; the centralization of control mechanisms) and the use of power as an agent of change (e.g., to modify one or several aspects of the context in which power is being applied, be they physical, economic, military, social, or diplomatic). Obviously, the borderline between these two possible functions of power is fre-

quently a tenuous one; indeed, the two are not necessarily
exclusive of one another. To a considerable extent, the
political history of modern capitalist societies may be
viewed as one that illustrates the use of change as an
instrument of power regeneration. In the contemporary
African context, much the same observation may be said
to apply to quite a few economic development projects, to
the creation of a good number of governmental agencies,
to the swelling of army ranks and the purchase of
military hardware, to the reorganization (or, as the case
may be, the preservation) of traditional authority systems
—not to mention such limited doses of change as pay
raises and fringe benefits. Since self-perpetuation is a
primary function of political systems and of institutionalized power, it seems hardly surprising that African governments, regardless of their ideological epidermis,
should look upon change and modernization as instruments of stability. Thus, economic development and
modernization find themselves subjected not only to the
degree of economic and societal transformability of the
country in which they take place, but also to the capability of the *political* structures to weather, to absorb,
and, *au besoin*, to anticipate change.

None of the new African states has been in existence
long enough to make it possible for an analyst to determine with any reasonable accuracy to what extent their
political systems possess this capability, although the few
elements which can be gathered so far seem to indicate
that it is rather limited. A key factor in this respect may
be the lack of any widespread identification between the
political oligarchy and the economic oligarchy in the
newly independent states of sub-Saharan Africa. Economic power remains, by and large, firmly entrenched in
the hands of foreign interest groups, and no serious effort
has been made, so far, to alter the situation except, in a

limited way, as a form of reprisals against the deliberately hostile policy of an industrialized country (as in
Guinea). We are therefore faced in sub-Saharan Africa
with the somewhat uneasy coexistence of two power elites
functioning at different levels, basically incapable of
merging (since one of them is an alien group), and
showing no signs of absorbing one another.

Various patterns of relationship between these two elites
are theoretically conceivable. One would be that which
implies the subservience of the political elite to the economic elite. This is probably best illustrated by the
example of Katanga and can also be said to apply,
perhaps to a lesser extent, to Gabon and Mauritania.
Conversely, the submission of the economic elite to the
political elite represents the theoretical pecking order
suggested by the doctrine of most African political
parties. It is also the solution subsumed in the many
references to African socialism, or reflected in the reluc-
tance on the part of many African governments to see
Western economic aid result, through the exclusive promotion of private enterprise, in the development of an
autochthonous entrepreneurial class—a development believed to lead in turn to the dislocation of the officially
"classless" African society.

Yet another pattern of relationship between the political
and the economic elite is that which would result from the
gradual interpenetration of the two oligarchies. There are,
in theory at least, several ways by which this interpenetration might be achieved, but the only one which appears
really practicable is the development of an indigenous
entrepreneurial class—an African bourgeoisie capable of
eventually replacing non-African interests. One cannot
help but entertain serious doubts, however, as to the
economic credibility and the political implications of such
a development. The gap between the emergence of even a

modest African bourgeoisie (not merely a middle class of
relatively affluent, salaried white-collar workers) and the
financial means of the alien interest groups remains
obviously too large to be bridged within the foreseeable
future. Furthermore, the assumption in some Western
circles that the development of an African entrepreneurial
class would automatically lead to the type of liberal
institutions which accompanied the Industrial Revolution
in parts of Western Europe is, to say the least, highly
questionable. The equation of private enterprise with
political democratization is confronted, in the case of
Africa (as in the case of several European states) with
the fact that the indigenous politico-economic elite would
have no direct stake in the democratization of the political
system. The example of the landed oligarchies of Latin
America and of their relationship with foreign enterprise
offers interesting parallels in this respect.

Finally, a fourth possible pattern of relationship between the political and economic elites postulates mutual
respect for one another's positions, as is presently the case
in virtually every new African state. It is, however, a type
of relationship which offers dubious stability in the hypothesis of an economic contraction which generates
popular discontent susceptible of being articulated as a
political challenge to the established order. Furthermore,
even assuming the absence of an economic disruption,
this situation contains the seeds of considerable political
instability. If the economic sources of power are to
remain, for all practical purposes, beyond the reach of the
most dynamic autochthonous groups, competition for
those political functions that are tangential to economic
activity and profit is likely to be quite strong. In return
for extending to the foreign-owned interests the seal of
legitimacy which national sovereignty of the African state
formally requires, the political class gains access to vari-

ous forms of economic gratification and tends to become, in the eyes of the foreign entrepreneur, an item of expenditure justified (like air-conditioning equipment) by the local conditions of business. A perceptive analyst of Latin America has diagnosed the relationship between economic and political power in terms that apply almost word for word to the African context:

Because of the colonial nature of the . . . economies, an exceptional economic premium attaches to control of the apparatus of government as a dynamic base of power. . . . Chronic political instability is a function of the contradiction between the realities of a colonial economy and the political requirements of legal sovereignty. . . . The pattern of political instability, significantly, has not evolved as a challenge to the conventional economic bases of power. . . . Chronic political instability serves as an avenue of socio-economic mobility, but it does not pose a genuine danger to the control of the conventional economic bases of power.[6]

The foregoing analysis suggests two general observations that reflect on the problems of political stability in Africa. First, the importance of institutional control, of ✳ *imperium,* of organized normative and coercive action as factors of political cohesion has tended to increase in the independent states of Africa, to the relative detriment of political socialization and mobilization such as were carried out by the political parties during the period of anti-colonial struggle. Second, the continued dichotomy between political control and economic control in terms of opportunities attaches a considerable incentive to the seizure of political power (and conversely, to the retention of such power by those who already hold it), thus endangering political stability, though only within certain limits.

The emphasis placed upon the institutionalized aspects of political power magnifies the role of the instruments of

organized authority, most prominent of which are the
military and the bureaucracy. While the politician may
remain the "cultural hero" of modernizing African societies, there is little doubt that the local party militant, for
instance, increasingly finds himself overshadowed by the
bearers of authority symbols derived not from the party,
but from the government. Admittedly, a considerable
degree of confusion persists in the identification by the
local population of the legitimacy of sources of authority.
Is the African head of state obeyed *qua* President of the
Republic or because of his charismatic virtues—or because he represents a combination of both forms of
legitimacy? Is the local administrator accepted because he
derives his legitimacy from an African government, because he is a native son of the district he administers (if
such be the case), or because he may be an old nationalist
militant who has changed hats? The closer one comes to
the summit of the political hierarchy, however, the
greater is the identification of power with the office held
in the state apparatus and with the legal symbols of
authority. Within this framework of modern ascriptive
values, high-ranking members of the armed forces (army
and police) and of the civil service are in a position to
wield a substantial amount of influence and power, and
thus to compete for the rewards of political control.

The validity of the above remarks is illustrated most
strikingly in the case of the Congo. While the Congo has
admittedly known a number of uncharacteristic vicissitudes, the very deficiencies of its central political structures magnify the role of subordinate power centers (such
as the army, the police, or the bureaucracy) in the
absence of popularly based, or at least popularly accepted, political leadership. Whereas power in the colonial

Congo was based on the sometimes uneasy but nevertheless effective cooperation of the colonial bureaucracy, the large business groups, and the missionary circles, no group or coalition can be said to be in stable control today. I have argued elsewhere[7] that most of the Congo's problems can be analyzed in terms of this "power vacuum" and stem more or less immediately from a lack of direction or from the absence of an articulated relay between pressures/demands and the social and economic cadres which often continue to operate at their functional level. Improvised responses by local or functional agencies, while not necessarily intended to challenge the authority of the central institutions, nevertheless tend to undermine this authority, or at least to negate its claims to unrestricted competence by tending toward the establishment of new decision-making circuits.

In a moment of unguarded frankness, the former commander of the Congolese *Force Publique*, General Janssens, described the force he had once said would be "the backbone" of the new Congo in the following rather unflattering terms: ". . . Who was sent into the Force Publique? The least promising individuals, the pupils who had been expelled from school, the refuse of the nation."[8] Although the general's description referred to the force as he found it in the mid-fifties, his comment might well apply to a good portion of the Congolese National Army, as the former colonial force is now designated. The ANC (*Armée Nationale Congolaise*) numbers over 30,000 men and its budget represents more than one fourth of the total national expenditure. At one time (the end of 1960) there were at least 40,000 men under arms in four antagonistic armies: that of the Léopoldville authorities, under Mobutu (15,000); the Katanga "gendarmerie" (12,000); a Lumumbist army under General Lundula (10,000 men); and a smaller force in Albert Kalonji's secessionist state of South Kasai —not to mention, of course, the UN contingent. To the current strength of the ANC should also be added some 15,000 police and security forces; for, as William Gutteridge perceptively pointed out,[9] the functional distinction between the army and the police which has been institutionalized in virtually all stable, developed nations loses much of its significance in Africa and other underdeveloped areas of the world.

Like almost all other countries of Africa, the Congo has yet to face any serious menace of external aggression, although it has had to cope with severe cases of internal disruption—some of them actually sparked by the army itself. But while taking no real part in the reunification of the country, the Congolese armed forces have played a major role in eliminating all forms of articulate opposition for the benefit of whichever political group managed to secure their loyalty—be it entrenched in Léopoldville, Elisabethville, Stanleyville, or Bakwanga. As a rule, the former Force Publique took quite naturally to this role, since it was consistent with its traditional mission of maintaining law and order internally rather than warding off nonexistent invaders. Under Belgian rule, the Force Publique, like other colonial armed forces, had reached a high degree of proficiency in disciplining troubled areas; "pacifying" restless tribes; and persuading uncooperative chiefs, religious zealots, or tax delinquents. The ruthlessness of these "military promenades," as they were euphemistically named, was largely ensured by an unswerving adherence to the cardinal principle of colonial security forces: never to quarter native troops in their own tribal homeland. The brutality exhibited by the ANC under

Lumumba toward the civilian populations of Kasai, and under Mobutu toward those of Kwilu, or by the Katangese gendarmerie toward the Luba of northern Katanga testifies to the unimpaired competence of Congolese forces to deal with internal situations. Obviously, however, governmental forces are far from conforming to Mao Tsetung's precept that "the army should be among the people as a fish swimming in the water." In the three regions mentioned above, military intervention resulted not in stamping out the rebellious movements, but rather in driving the local peasantry to identify and solidarize with the insurgents.[10] It is an interesting reflection upon the handling of internal security problems that the local constabulary of the rebellious Kwilu province had to be disbanded because of its alleged unreliability.[11]

But while it may not have been entirely successful in coping with mass disturbances, the Congolese army—or at least fractions thereof—have been used most effectively by a small number of individuals to alter, hamstring, or nullify the normal functioning of political and constitutional institutions. Troops surrounded the parliament building when Lumumba sought a vote of confidence from the legislature in his conflict with Kasavubu. Later in the same month of September 1960, Colonel (later General) Mobutu moved on to the political scene at the head of a small but rugged detachment of loyal soldiers to announce his intention of "neutralizing" all political authorities in the country—a façade of impartiality which he abandoned in a matter of weeks. In Stanleyville, the gradual disaffection of the army under General Lundula was the most important single factor in the withering of the Gizenga regime. The army also played a key role in the arrest and subsequent release of Moïse Tshombe, in silencing the Lumumbist parliamentary opposition and in

driving its most radical members into clandestine action,
as well as in the outcome of a score of relatively obscure
power struggles which took place outside of Léopoldville.

It is in the capital itself, however, that the political
leverage of military pressure is the most effective: we
have noted earlier the importance of control over the
formal machinery of state power where popular mobilization and a transcending national consciousness are lacking. For this reason, the creation by Mobutu (with the
help of the Moroccan General Kettani) of a small,
intensely loyal force of eight hundred paratroopers was a
development of enormous political significance. Charac-
teristically, the political influence of this battalion (com-
manded by Colonel Tshatshi, later appointed Chief of
Staff to replace Colonel Ebaya, killed in action in Kwilu)
is totally unrelated to its effectiveness in restoring law and
order in the interior, since it seldom leaves its quarters
around Mobutu's residence at Binza (a suburb of Léopoldville). Mobutu's strength in Léopoldville is also bolstered by the presence at Thysville (one hundred miles
west of the capital) of another faithful unit, an armored
brigade formerly under the command of an old career
officer, Colonel Bobozo, who was Mobutu's instructor ten
years ago.

Another key element of political power on the Léopoldville scene is the internal security police known as the *Sûreté*. A pervasive instrument of Belgian colonial rule, it
has been since 1960 the object of some of the fiercest
conflicts of influence. One of Kasavubu's very first moves
after revoking Lumumba was to replace the former Prime
Minister's appointee by a known enemy of Lumumba,
Victor Nendaka. Even more than Mobutu, Nendaka was
responsible for the wholesale persecution of Lumumbist
elements in Léopoldville between September 1960 and the

inauguration of the Adoula government. There is also every reason to believe that he was one of the prime movers of the decision to have the deposed premier assassinated. Adoula, who was Minister of the Interior at the time of Lumumba's murder, made futile attempts to assert his control over the Sûreté, as did his successor, Gbenye, when Adoula became Prime Minister. In this latter instance, Gbenye's order dismissing Nendaka was simply ignored by the chief of the Sûreté; Mobutu immediately concurred by dispatching a group of his faithful bodyguards to prevent Nendaka from being forcibly dislodged. Thereafter, Nendaka's position as one of the major power brokers and political arbiters in Léopoldville remained largely unchallenged. It may be safely assumed that one of the chief factors of Nendaka's influence and invulnerability lies in his privileged access to the extensive and frequently damaging information accumulated by his services on the activities of several members of the political oligarchy.

The future role of the armed and security forces (which, for the purposes of our discussion, can be lumped together) on the Congolese political scene is difficult to estimate—except for the safe prediction that it will, in all likelihood, be considerable. Yet, beyond securing for themselves the most exorbitant pay raises[12] and acting as instruments of the anti-Lumumbist circles in Léopoldville, they have achieved amazingly little constructive action toward the goals of political stability and nation-building. This shortcoming may be linked with the nature of the Congolese armed forces themselves, or perhaps with the very essence of military rule. Certainly, the military is, in the words of Edward Shils:

. . . capable of playing a constructive part in the provision of some of the elements of a modern, and even democratic, society. It can serve to integrate diverse ethnic groups into

a national community; it can teach skills useful in economic
development; it can widen horizons beyond village and locality; it can keep young men from being infected by nationalistic demagogy and give them a greater concern for the nation as a whole.[13]

The Congolese armed forces, however, fall short of these
tasks on almost every count. Not only are they the direct
descendants of an instrument of colonial policy which
took absolutely no part in the brief struggle for independence (as opposed, for example, to the Algerian army),
but despite Mobutu's pronouncements at the time of his
1960 *Putsch,* they have failed to maintain even the sem-
blance of political neutrality—an essential ingredient in
military claims to be "above party politics." The total
absence of an autochthonous officer corps is being hastily
remedied, but the sort of *esprit de corps* acquired in the
great military academies by many officers of the Indian
or Moroccan armies will presumably remain lacking for
some time.

Yet whether or not the armed forces are socially and
psychologically ripe for a take-over, the almost fatalistic
prediction of many observers is that they will be drawn
into direct political action as a result of Adoula's failure
to fill the power vacuum in Léopoldville. The army may
indeed be biding its time in a slightly rear-stage position:
unlike the Adoula regime, which fights for survival by an
almost daily reshuffle of its bases of power, it can afford
to wait and even expect time to play into its hands as the
date scheduled for the withdrawal of UN forces draws
closer. The apparent inevitability of praetorian intervention in the Congo does not, however, necessarily guar-
antee enduring political stability. The entanglement of
certain sections of the army in party intrigue has its
counterpart in the vulnerability of its officer corps to political infiltration—not to mention sheer opportunism. Two

recent cases of military mutiny—one at Luluabourg in October 1963 during which some two hundred officers and men were won over by anti-governmental propaganda, the other, which nearly cost Mobutu and Nendaka their lives, at the end of December 1963—testify to the continued fragility of military cohesiveness. Since the time of independence, the military has been, at best, an instrument of political coercion and repression in the hands of an insecure oligarchy and, at worst, an uncontrolled golem-like force capable of destructive, but not constructive, political action. Increased military influence over the political apparatus may be expected to produce within a fairly short time the type of regime that has been characterized by one analyst as "government without authority"[14]; in other words, the "praetorian state." In his concise description of the praetorian state, David C. Rapoport depicts a polity strongly reminiscent of the contemporary Congo:

To the outside observer, praetorian politics seem "formless," for the government of the day is not sustained by strong sentiments or well-disciplined social groups that enable it to weather adversity or to pursue consistent policies. Even governments which appear reasonably secure will fall suddenly in response to a slight change of circumstance. . . . Usually only a strong personality can secure momentary stability, but he rarely produces the institutions to confirm an appropriate successor. Swollen, rootless and *idle* urban mobs complicate the problem of governing. . . . The army is the most fruitful source for political intrigue, and the government conspires to promote its military supporters, while the opposition attempts to curry favor with the most strategically placed military men. The officer corps invariably attracts two distinct political types—the political adventurer willing to gamble all in a dangerous stroke and the petty bureaucrat anxious to hold his rank in successive regimes and, therefore, reluctant to proceed vigorously against

a rebel group. The rank and file who must suppress urban
riots are drawn from politically "innocent" groups. . . .
The political situation makes it impossible to organize an
army with real fighting qualities. . . . Behind defensive
barricades, the army may be able to hold its own, but little
ability is displayed in the field. The state . . . will fight few
wars in any case. . . . Even a successful military campaign
. . . introduces an extra element of uncertainty in domestic
politics.[15]

The situation outside of Léopoldville is already deterio-
rating to a point where military rule in the capital may fit
even more closely the description of the above model.
Forms of insurgency such as that which has been developing in the Kwilu area seem to exhibit the type of populist–
nihilist rejection of authority which the military is, almost congenitally, incapable of understanding, suppressing, or controlling. The *raison d'être* of military rule is
primarily its capacity to restore law and order. Faced
with widespread insurgency, it almost invariably over-
reacts and embarks upon the form of repression that fuels
the rebellion. A revolt such as that in Kwilu can of course
be physically suppressed—it has been done before—and
the amount of support which the rebels can expect from
outside sources is sharply limited. The threat that the
rebellion implies for Léopoldville and for the Congolese
economy (for example, by cutting the rail–river export
route of Katanga copper) may indeed precipitate the
trend toward more permanent military rule in the capital
(as opposed to the declaration of a temporary state of
emergency as in December 1963), but such a development would not by itself endow the military with states-
manship. Assuming that the army can, with the continued
assistance of Western countries,[16] surmount its organizational and functional deficiencies and become a tightly
knit, highly efficient instrument, a military oligarchy

would still face the problems inherent in this type of regime. As Edward Shils points out:

Like all elites, that of a military oligarchy must demonstrate its effectiveness if it is to retain its position. The easiest ways to manifest its effectiveness are by vigor in suppressing attempted *Putsches*, cleaning up streets, removing beggars from the center of the main towns, prosecuting the beneficiaries of the preceding regime, and preventing the spread of rumors of corruption about its own regime. It can do these things quite successfully. Military elites suffer from the disadvantage that, once they have succeeded in these undertakings, there is not much more that they can do to support their own self-confidence and to impress themselves on the public mind. . . . To summarize: the military oligarchy is not a complete regime. It has neither a comprehensive program, nor a perspective into the future. Like all nonhereditary oligarchies, it has no provision for succession. It is what some of the military oligarchs themselves call a "caretaker regime." But its ideas about what it takes care of are rather scant and, even where well-intentioned, unimaginative.[17]

When General Mobutu (then a Colonel) made his first appearance on the political scene in September 1960, he announced in the same breath the "neutralization" of all political institutions and his intention to call upon the handful of Congolese university graduates to run the administrative machinery of the new republic, thus sealing an alliance that continues to dominate the political horizon while at the same time acknowledging a truth discerned long ago by political scientists: namely that military rule cannot endure without a minimum of cooperation from the bureaucracy. In the colonial context, the association—indeed, the identification—of soldiers and functionaries was always particularly close: from Lugard to Liautey, the first administrators were almost invariably military men. Moreover, in the case of Belgian Africa, the

administration had always been the nerve center of the
colonial system. As Raymond Buell had already noted in
the 1920's, no other territory on the continent was so
thoroughly or so densely administered as the Belgian
Congo.[18] Contrary to the Force Publique, which never
was considered an outlet for intellectually agile Africans,
the colonial civil service attracted virtually all the best-
educated Congolese. Yet on the eve of independence only
three Congolese had reached the top three levels of the
administrative hierarchy (the corresponding number of
Belgians for these three grades was 4,642), while at the
fourth level of the civil service, where Africans and
expatriates were in more direct competition, there were
only some 800 Congolese as against 5,159 Belgians.[19]
Nevertheless, the bureaucratic character of the Congolese
elite is best illustrated by the fact that 66 of the 137
deputies and 31 of the 84 senators in the Congolese
parliament of 1960 were public employees.[20]

These figures should not, however, convey the idea that
the Congolese bureaucracy is a highly politicized body.
True, there was no equivalent to the sharp line drawn by
the British between the civil service and the political
parties in the English-speaking states of Africa (a line
which, incidentally, is becoming increasingly blurred in
the case of most of them), but the Belgian colonial
administration had strong traditions of noninvolvement
in political activity, this being in turn the consequence of
the consistent Belgian policy of denying political rights to
all persons residing in the Congo, whatever their race or
nationality. The massive exodus of Congolese civil servants into the political arena between 1958 and 1960 was
merely a result of the scarcity of intellectual elites and of
the limited opportunities of promotion offered by the
colonial administration until the very last days of Belgian
rule.

Since 1960, however, a reverse trend has become apparent, and the bureaucracy rather than the parties attract the best-educated Congolese, the growing number of university graduates; in short, most of the able and promising members of the younger generation. A similar phenomenon has been observed in other parts of Africa and competition for the intellectual elite between the party cadres and the civil service increasingly tends to favor the latter.[21] In the Congo, this trend is reinforced by the gradual decay of political parties after independence, and by the sheer physical risks of political action. The momentary failure of political parties as avenues to power and influence has diverted many educated Congolese into the ranks of the administration, where they feel they can safely wait for a change in political prospects. The bureaucracy thus becomes a refuge for the intellectual elite. As mentioned earlier, it has also fallen heir to a considerable amount of effective power, partly as a result of the lack of political direction, and partly as a result of the unchallenged colonial tradition of bureaucratic control.

It would be misleading, however, to deal with bureaucratic influence as a monolithic force in the contemporary Congo. The bureaucracy is no more of a homogeneous group than the military—indeed, probably less so. The top ranks of the civil service, whether competent or not, exercise only a limited effective control outside of the capital. Yet, as in the case of Mobutu's praetorian guard, their influence over the central government machinery is considerable, and no political group can hope to maintain itself in power without a minimum of support or cooperation from the high-ranking bureaucrats. Outside of Léopoldville, however, a considerable amount of *de facto* decentralization has taken place since 1960. The loosening of institutional and functional links between the capital and the rest of the country has strained the lines of command to the point where they frequently have snapped. The result has been a relaxation of the colonial tradition of direct, centralized rule and uniform policy. Despite numerous attempts by Léopoldville to re-establish hierarchical control by the appointment of "special" or "extraordinary" commissioners to supervise and, on occasion, redress the action of local civil servants, guarantees against the arbitrary measures of a local administrator are still far from being totally effective. On the other hand, the local administrator himself frequently has no certainty that his word will be obeyed by the local population unless he can advance some additional claim to authority—such as being a native son, or being able to count on the backing of the nearest detachment of the armed forces. In a few cases, traditional authorities simply expelled the government-appointed administrator and restored customary normative and administrative mechanisms.[22]

Despite its current fragmentation, the bureaucracy undeniably exercises considerable power by default, both in Léopoldville and at the provincial level. The judgment made by a perceptive observer in December 1962 that "the mandarins are in command"[23] remains largely valid today, but the question of whether the administration could "develop the national outlook and innovating capacity which parties have inspired elsewhere in Africa," raised by the same author, is still very much in doubt. While the bureaucracy can probably weather any change of regime and retain the power it currently wields, its ability to initiate or orient such a change or to supplement failing political leadership appears highly questionable.

There are, on the contrary, strong indications that the expanding role of the bureaucracy in a developing country may inhibit, rather than assist, the growth of strong or active political institutions. Whether in a "modernizing autocracy" or in a post-colonial polity, the traditions of strong, uncontrolled executive action tend to place the bureaucracy in a position of unrestrained power. The increasing emphasis on developmental tasks of a highly technical nature places a premium on professional skills and administrative competence rather than on securing popular participation in the formulation and implementation of national goals. But while they are of great intrinsic importance, the problems of efficiency and of professional ethics are not central to the purpose of our discussion. The ideal norms of Weberian bureaucracy are, in most cases, totally irrelevant in the context of an underdeveloped country, and great effectiveness of performance can be achieved in contradiction to the more or less rationalized norms evolved by Western administrative systems. Of greater importance for the subject of this inquiry, however, is the long-term role that a bureaucracy can perform in the emergence of a viable polity. In the best circumstances, the administrators "helped to maintain the framework of a unified polity as well as the capacity to absorb varied demands and to regulate them effectively, . . . enabled the rulers to implement continuous policy . . . [and] served as important instruments for the mobilization of resources—taxes, manpower and political support."[24] Not only does the bureaucracy "play a part in setting up, determining and implementing political goals as well as in establishing major policy directives," but it also tends to develop as a major instrument of social change and as "one of the main channels of political struggle in which and through which different interests are regulated and aggregated."[25] Contrasting with this ideally positive model of an abstract bureaucracy—many elements of which could not, in any case, be found in today's Congo—comes the warning that "prema-

ture or too rapid expansion of the bureaucracy when the
political system lags behind tends to inhibit the development of effective politics."[26] The same author suggests
that "without firm political guidance, bureaucrats have
weak incentives to provide good service . . . [and] tend
to use their effective control to safeguard their expedient
bureaucratic interests—tenure, seniority rights, fringe
benefits, toleration of poor performance, the right to
violate official norms—rather than to advance the achievement of program goals. . . . Hence, [he adds] the
career, merit bureaucracy in a developing country not
only fails to accomplish the administrative goals set for it
but also stands in the way of political growth."[27]

A reorganized, restructured Congolese bureaucracy can
undoubtedly have a deep and lasting influence on the
development of normative patterns of behavior which
transcend the limits of kinship, village, or ethnic ties: in
doing so, actually, it would only carry on—and probably
perfect—the integrative process initiated by the Belgian
colonial administration which, after all, was the prime
instrumental force that led a number of men to identify
themselves for the first time as "Congolese." It appears
improbable, however, that the bureaucracy should be
able—or willing—to play a major role in developing
mechanisms of consensus formation, the most visible
result of which, from its viewpoint, would be to intensify
popular demands and pressures and to open up channels
of control over the executive. Spontaneous self-limitation
of the executive has never been known to be a widely
practiced or realistic safeguard against arbitrary rule. In
a conflict (be it even an institutionalized or sublimated
conflict) between the leaders and the led, the bureaucracy
has not been in the habit of siding with the latter group.
If political stability is equated with continuity of executive action, the contribution of the bureaucracy can be of

inestimable value; if, on the other hand, it is founded on
the diffusion of power among an increasingly wide popular base through integrative political devices, its role is
likely to be limited and possibly negative. It should be
remembered, nevertheless, that these two concepts of
political stability are not bound to be mutually exclusive.

It has been repeatedly submitted—perhaps by now *ad
nauseam*—that political parties play a crucial, or at the
least a catalytic, role in the related phenomena of stability
and change in developing countries. As the foregoing
discussion tended to suggest, however, it may be that too
much importance has been attached to political parties in
the study of Africa, particularly to the tentative taxonomy
which opposes mass parties to *partis de cadres*. While this
distinction has been extremely useful during the era of
national liberation, current evidence would tend to suggest that parties, once in power, tend to behave in a
similar fashion. They may also tend to lose some of their
usefulness, at least as far as the power elite is concerned.
African political parties were organized, as a rule, in a
spirit of change: usually to promote such change, occasionally to take advantage of it, but in any case with the
underlying assumption that change would benefit the
people—and, by implication, the party members. The
forms of change advocated in the days of colonial rule
were commonly undifferentiated. Parties frequently made
use of the vocabulary of social and economic protest
developed by non-African parties of the post-nationalist
era—usually the Marxist parties, and occasionally the
Fascist ones—but, without much exception, their actual
tactics were oriented toward political and institutional
change rather than toward social and economic transformations. The visible and tangible goal of eliminating
imperial rule absorbed most of the energies of African

political parties up to the time of independence. In several
countries, the party's struggle for a monopoly of power
coincided with the efforts to attain this goal and was
achieved simultaneously with it. In others, the former
struggle went on after independence and the establishment
of a single or dominant party became more closely
associated with the institutional framework of the state. A
good example of this functional confusion is the Central
African Republic, where members of the national bureau
of the MESAN (*Mouvement pour l'Évolution Sociale de
l'Afrique Noire*) were elevated by law to the rank of
salaried public officials.[28]

Few parties, however, have been able, once power had
been conquered, to maintain the momentum achieved
during the struggle for independence, or the degree of
popular mobilization they had succeeded in establishing
during the terminal period of colonial rule. The reasons
for this situation have already been touched upon: the
fact that militancy is easier to obtain in pursuit of the
relatively simple and emotionally charged task of ousting
the alien ruler than for the more sustained and less visibly
rewarding tasks of development; the increasing preoccupation of a number of *nantis* with preservation of the
political *status quo*—and consequently with security and
police problems; the fact that developmental tasks increasingly pass into the hands of technocrats rather than
into those of the party rank and file; and also that most
African governments, although (or rather because) they
depend on foreign sources of development capital, seldom
challenge very seriously the continued existence of economic privilege. Thus the most active parties today are
those which have yet to establish their monopoly over
state power, while "sated" parties tend to fall into a
relative state of lethargy. One may even envisage (though

with several important reservations) the eventual passage from the one-party to the no-party state.

The Congo has skipped entirely the stage during which the nationalist parties assert their claim to power through the fight for national independence—or rather, this stage was so brief that its usual effects were atrophied or at least diluted. For this reason, political life in the Congo may never conform to the patterns observed in other sub-Saharan countries. The only Congolese party with a tenuous claim to national leadership (MNC-Lumumba) was overthrown by a conjunction of domestic and alien forces before it could assert its hold over the state machinery and use it to enforce conformity. It also lost in Patrice Lumumba the only politician with the demonstrated capacity of eliciting mass support and consensus.

Since 1960, political power, like the spirit of God in the first chapter of Genesis, has been floating above the waters of intrigue and of anarchy tempered by coercion. All successive regimes—whether legal or not—have been too engrossed in the problem of reshuffling their inconsistent bases of support *in* Léopoldville to set about the task of seeking permanent bases of support *outside* of the capital. As a result, each of them (including, it would now seem, the Adoula government) has been little more than a *cabinet de coulisses*, i.e. one which relies on maneuverings conducted in the aisles and backrooms— formerly those of parliament and, now that parliament has proved intractable and has been, for all practical purposes, dissolved, those of the major power brokers, the men who control the army, the police, the security services, or the channels of communication with friendly foreign powers. Repeatedly, but with indifferent success, attempts were made by the Adoula government to broaden its base of support by making advances toward the labor movement, the Lumumbist opposition, and the regional "barons" such as Tshombe. After having exhausted the range of possible power combinations, Adoula now finds it increasingly difficult to rearrange the pieces of the Léopoldville political kaleidoscope in a way that might leave him less exclusively dependent on the core of Congolese political power: the "Binza group."[29]

Since the beginning of 1964, there have been alarming signs that an increasingly large number of political circles are gambling on Adoula's downfall—and, possibly, on the chaos which might ensue. The setting up by the radical wing of the Lumumbist parties of a Committee of National Liberation (CNL) in Brazzaville is probably the most obvious of these signs. Though rent by intestine quarrels and reluctant at first to become publicly associated with Pierre Mulele, the CNL apparently decided that it could get some political mileage out of the Kwilu rebellion—as well as from similar upheavals which it has been trying to kindle in other areas of the Congo.

Slightly more recently, the apparent breakdown in the occult, protracted attempts to achieve a rapprochement between Adoula and Tshombe, triggered by the latter's publication of a version of Lumumba's murder which is highly damaging to many Léopoldville politicians, has raised speculations that the former Katanga president might be trying to seal an alliance of extremes against the Léopoldville "center." This interpretation gains support from the fact that it was in a pro-Lumumbist Belgian periodical that Mr. Tshombe's exculpation was first publicized, and that Lumumbist circles were surprisingly uncritical in their acceptance of the self-exonerating assertions of their onetime archenemy.[30] Another possible explanation of Mr. Tshombe's attitude is that it is aimed exclusively at the politically ailing Adoula but does not jeopardize the possibility of a subsequent rapprochement with President Kasavubu and the Binza group, should the Premier be eased out in the near future. The credibility of this alternative interpretation is bolstered by the fact that Harry Nkumbula's opposition party in Northern Rhodesia, the African National Congress, which is known to have close links with the former secessionist regime of Katanga, staged a demonstration against Mr. Adoula when the latter attended the formal opening of the Northern Rhodesian parliament, charging the Congolese Premier alone with the murder of Patrice Lumumba.[31] The weak link in this version of Mr. Tshombe's tactics is that it would appear to be virtually impossible to blame Lumumba's murder on Mr. Adoula alone without running the risk of implicating at least some members of the Binza group, and possibly President Kasavubu himself—a consequence that might destroy the alleged purpose of Tshombe's "disclosures."

Finally, in what amounts to a more insidious challenge, the adoption of a constitutional project by an *ad hoc* drafting commission convened in Luluabourg at the invitation of President Kasavubu has paved the way for a thoroughgoing institutional reform that could sharply curtail Adoula's powers and, circumstantially, eliminate him (though not the office he holds) from the political stage. Though patently annoyed by the obstructional tactics of the national parliament, which is the only body legally qualified to draw up the new constitution, the Prime Minister was reportedly piqued by the President's decision to convene a large (125 members) pseudo-parliamentary drafting commission which he immediately set about to endow with a special legitimacy.[32] The drafting commission—which, incidentally, included representatives of the provincial assemblies but *not* of the national parliament—thereupon laid claim to being a veritable constituent assembly by expressing the wish to

see the project it was supposed to draft "submitted as
such to a popular referendum without being subjected to
any modification"[33]—a direct challenge to the amending
powers of both the national parliament and the cabinet.
The rift between the Adoula cabinet and the presidential
drafting commission was further stressed when the commission decided to adopt as the starting point of its
deliberations the draft prepared in 1962 by an international team of jurists rather than—as had initially been
understood—the somewhat more centralizing project submitted at the end of 1963 by the Adoula cabinet.

Mr. Adoula's misgivings were presumably reinforced
by the declarations made by the chairman of the constitutional commission, Mr. Ileo, upon submitting the constitutional draft to the President. Mr. Ileo announced that
President Kasavubu would automatically remain the head
of the new presidential system for a period of at least
sixteen months following the adoption of the constitution
by popular referendum, whereas Mr. Adoula's cabinet
would have to resign upon promulgation of the constitution to give way to a new cabinet. Mr. Ileo went on to add
that this new cabinet "might be, for example, the present
government remodeled after the spirit of the Luluabourg
charter. But Mr. Kasavubu has the possibility of calling
upon another *formateur* than Mr. Adoula."[34] Another
spokesman for the constitutional commission delivered a
more direct attack against the Prime Minister by criticiz-
ing Mr. Adoula's announced intention of taking up the
constitutional project in the cabinet for further examination and possible amendment "merely in order to hang on
to power and perpetuate the crisis."[35] While he did not go
so far as to question the Premier's right to initiate
amendments, which was spelled out in the ordinance
setting up the commission, he warned against the possi-

bility of "unfortunate consequences" should the cabinet attempt to modify the Luluabourg draft.

Apart from the fact that the Congo has long been in need of a permanent constitution (it is nominally subject at this writing to the interim Fundamental Law voted by the Belgian parliament shortly before independence), the chief political value of the proposed charter, from the viewpoint of the Léopoldville oligarchy, is that it disposes for another ten months of the nagging problem of the next congressional elections, which should normally have been held in May 1964 and the approach of which had provoked the anxiety of the members of the new ruling class. With the day of reckoning now postponed until March 1965 the Congolese oligarchy won another breathing spell and thus momentarily solved the problem of political stability. It remains to be seen what means it proposes to adopt in order to extend its lease on power beyond its next deadline. Will it use the respite to plant more firmly the roots of autocracy, or will it follow the more arduous path of trying to evoke a true popular consensus? Or could it be engulfed in a swell of popular anger? Of these three eventualities, the latter is by no means the most improbable.

*   *   *

This paper was completed in April, 1964. Since that time, a number of developments have contributed to bring the Congo back into the headlines; these developments also provide an appropriate postscript to my analysis of the Congo situation. I have, therefore, refrained from altering or updating the contents of my paper; in doing

*so, of course, I deliberately denied myself the benefit of
the delay which separates thought from print and, hence,
rejected the tempting opportunity to sharpen or blur,
retrospectively, certain brush strokes for the sake of ex
post facto "coherence." A number of elements which were
already present on the Congolese scene in April, 1964, but
could not be included in my analysis because of their then
speculative character have since become considerably
more apparent; among these are the United States determination to intervene more openly in Congolese affairs,
and the existence of dissensions in the ranks of the
opposition. Other factors, such as the reappearance of
white "mercenaries," while apparently new, are in fact
the logical result of the rapid polarization of political
oppositions following Mr. Tshombe's access to power.*

In a number of ways, the formation of the Tshombe
government (the outcome of the dubious legal and political maneuvers described in the course of my paper) and
its subsequent policies have clarified the situation. The
precarious façade of national reconciliation, which had
been laboriously built by Mr. Adoula and had been
decaying for some months, has now been shattered. Rival
factions are further apart from each other than at any
time since 1961. More important, in addition to its
reliance upon its sponsors, the United States and Belgium,
the Tshombe regime has become increasingly dependent
upon the assistance of white soldiers of fortune, most of
them from the white-dominated areas of southern Africa:
indeed, virtually the only military successes scored
against the spreading rebellion have been the work of
these white commandos.

In its support of Mr. Tshombe the United States thus
finds itself in the company of strange bedfellows. Yet both
the United States and the white supremacists can point to
the logical coherence of their respective policies: the

official United States position is, roughly speaking, one of continued support for the central government of a united Congo, regardless of personalities, while on the other hand the policy line of South Africa, Portugal, and Rhodesia is based on continued support of Mr. Tshombe (and what he stands for), regardless of the office he holds. As for the attitude of the African states, it follows in reverse the internal logic of the position adopted by the white governments of southern Africa and it basically revolves around the same issues. This discrepancy between the United States and the African terms of reference highlights in retrospect the ambiguities that continually pervaded the conjunction of African and United States efforts to liquidate the Katanga secession. African opposition to the Katanga "state" was not only (or even primarily) directed against separatism as such but also against those features of the Elisabethville regime that are now re-emerging in Léopoldville, and which the United States does not appear to find antithetic to its support of Mr. Tshombe. This lack of a common denominator between the African and American appraisals of the Tshombe government would seem to be the most serious flaw for the long-term chances of success of United States policy in the Congo.

Apart from immediate problems of tactical success against the rebellion (which are being taken care of jointly by United States military assistance and white mercenary manpower), United States policy in the Congo suffers from three basic weaknesses. By deliberately choosing to overlook what Mr. Tshombe stands for, it tends to ignore the issues that are considered most crucial by a majority of African governments, whether black or white. Furthermore, the claim that United States support against Mr. Tshombe's adversaries is the logical continuation of the policy line which upheld the Adoula

government against the Katanga secessionists is largely
invalidated by the fact that the oppositional challenge to
the Léopoldville authorities is not directed against Congolese unity but against the regime—and, indeed, in the
case of most peasants, against "the system." Finally,
while ostensibly attaching considerable importance to the
somewhat disputable legality of the Tshombe government, United States policy pays insufficient attention
to the factor of legitimacy and to the related "capacity of the system to engender and maintain the belief that
the existing political institutions are the most appropriate
ones for the society."[36]

Clearly, the threat of Communist infiltration of the rebel
ranks has been a far more vital factor of United States
policy than any of the aforementioned rationalizations
of the American position offered by official circles. The
question, of course, remains whether Mr. Tshombe can
reasonably be considered as the most appropriate answer
to this threat and the most credible symbol of national
unity, or whether his advent to power as the result of ill-
concealed external backing will have the unwished-for
consequence of fulfilling what Ernesto "Che" Guevarra
regards as one of the necessary preconditions of successful subversive action, namely, that of "clearly demonstrat-
ing to the people the impossibility of maintaining the
struggle for social reforms within the framework of
legality."[37]

2

POLITICAL INFLUENCE

IN

SOUTHERN NIGERIA[1]

❦

HENRY L. BRETTON

Literature on modern governmental and political processes in tropical Africa has increased markedly in quan-
tity, but relatively little of it has provided empirical
support for mainly unsubstantiated generalizations. This
applies, among other areas of inquiry, to political influence as related to authoritative decision-making.[2]

For my purposes here, two major types of political
influence can be distinguished: broad, social, mass-based
influence that through a variety of diffuse channels makes
itself felt at the level of authoritative decision-making;
and the more easily ascertainable person-to-person influence that is exercised directly at strategic points in the
federal, regional, and local authoritative decision-making
centers. Whereas study of the former type, regardless of
the method employed, is bound to remain highly speculative, study of the latter can yield more reliable data more
readily, and can also yield meaningful insights into the
workings of the wider circles of social influence as repre-

sented by the sample selected for the survey. The present
survey, therefore, concerned itself mainly with the latter
type. Where appropriate, I also considered evidence of
political pressure and influence flowing downward from
the decision-makers and rulers generally, and tending to
affect, and probably impeding, the upward flow of influence.

Research for the present study was conducted in Southern Nigeria in the summer of 1963.* I hoped to attain
four central objectives, the fourth a long-range one:

1. Identification of a small sample of persons, and
through that sample of segments and groups of society,
that appeared to be endowed, actually or potentially, with
significant influence capabilities.

2. Analysis of the social bases and internal structure of
the segments and groups represented by the sample.

3. Evaluation of the segments and groups for their
influence potential in the specific context of authoritative
decision-making on critical socio-economic issues.

4. Development of an "anatomy" of the power and
influence structure in Southern Nigeria.

Influence, as here understood, refers to influence on a
person or persons who play significant roles in authoritative decision-making, as distinguished from derivative,
routine, marginal, bureaucratic, or purely administrative
decision-making.[3] Decisions of concern here are about
issues of direct, central, and critical relevance to the socio-
economic structure of the area under study; for example,
decisions about social or economic reform and development, resource allocation, management of political power,
and leadership recruitment.

* A discussion of the methods employed and the problems encountered in conducting the survey, and the questionnaire itself,
will be found in the Appendix, pages 171–188.

The major focus of the interviews was upon isolation of those persons and groups who seemed to exercise the greatest degree of influence upon key decision-makers, that is, who possessed greatest influence potential to secure legislative, administrative, or generally political satisfaction of their interests and demands. I expected they would include individual members of the ruling elite, persons who possessed influence potential in their own right, as well as groups specifically organized to represent interests of one kind or another and whose main purpose is to secure action on behalf of these interests at the several levels of government. Also expected to emerge from the survey were interest (or influence) groups spontaneously brought into being because of some dramatic occurrence, but whose longevity was likely to be limited.

The Political Situation at the Time of the Survey

Field research was conducted between June 18 and August 26, 1963. The survey coincided with preparations for the change-over from constitutional monarchy to federal republic. Accompanying these preparations were remarkably widespread and intense public discussions of matters related to the change. Foremost among the issues heatedly discussed in the press, at organized public meetings, and spontaneously in public places were rumored plans to establish a broader coalition government, provisions for what to the public at least appeared to be a "Preventive Detention Act" similar to the one enacted in Ghana in 1958, the independence of the judiciary, and in general the representative nature of the proposed constitutional system. The proposal to enact a measure enabling the federal government to hold in preventive detention persons suspected of treasonable activities was in part a response to the circumstances that had led to the then pending treason trial of Chief Awolowo and other leaders of the Action Group (AG). At the same time, a referendum was planned, campaigned for, and held to determine the future status of the Mid-West Region; this development suggested delay of my entry into the Mid-West until after the referendum.

Also of material relevance for my purposes were the conditions created in the Western Region by the forced collapse of the Action Group regime and by the emergence of a coalition of converted Action Group forces, then organized in the United People's Party (UPP) and the Western branch of the National Convention of Nigerian Citizens (NCNC). Responses clearly reflected what may be termed the injured sense of "national" pride of the Yorubas, dominant in the Western Region. Only the Eastern Region enjoyed at the time a relative state of stability, providing respondents there with a firmer base for influence evaluation.

Findings[4]

Political activity in Nigeria centers to a high degree on tribal interests; consequently, each of the major tribal groupings seeks political expression through a political party of its own. Thus the Hausa-Fulani grouping in the North organized the Northern People's Congress (NPC), the Yorubas of the West the Action Group (AG) and, later, its successor parties, and the Ibos of the East have their National Convention of Nigerian Citizens (NCNC). The NPC and the NCNC have formed the governing coalition at the federal level since independence.

I. EASTERN REGION

A. The National Convention of Nigerian Citizens (NCNC)

In the East, the NCNC appears to dominate the influence structure to the point where competing or generally independent sources of political influence are being reduced to the status of party appendages.*

Much of the evident popularity and strength at the polls of the NCNC can be traced to its identification with the party's founder, Dr. Azikiwe (formerly Governor General, now President of the Republic), and to the ready identification of the NCNC with Ibo "nationalism." Party representatives occupy all significant control points in state and society: the Premier's office, the Cabinet, the influential Eastern Nigeria Development Corporation, the equally influential African Continental Bank, the Marketing Boards. The party also dominates all local government, the one municipal council (Port Harcourt), the large and small urban county councils (Enugu, Umuahia, Aba, Onitsha, Owerri, etc.), and most of the county councils.[5] It also controls to varying degrees most of the Tender Boards, the Local Government Service Commissions, and by indirect means most of the traditional tribal systems.

Patronage at regional, municipal, and rural levels, contract awards, loans, regulatory powers over licensing, taxation, water rates, registration, extension or denial of amenities (roads, electrification, schools), threats of investigation and exposure, dissolution, and so on, are em-

* The present tense employed with regard to findings relates to the conditions prevailing at the time the interviews were conducted. It is not likely that the influence patterns described here have been altered significantly since research was completed.

ployed by the party leadership at all levels to influence
and control individuals and groups in all sectors of state
and society, public or private. This assures a virtual
Gleichschaltung of all actual and potential nonparty
sources of influence.[6]

Within the ruling segment in the NCNC, certain sub-
groups are given relative prominence and are endowed
with a certain power and influence potential, but more as
government instrumentalities than as autonomous sources
influencing the decision-makers independently. In Premier Okpara's office, in key party bodies, and on the
Boards, persons either from the Premier's own area,
Bende Division, or personally acceptable to him, are
favored. Increasingly, relatives and friends of traditional
and secular leaders from that area are found in key
positions in party and state. This development is attributed to the Premier's desire to replace the Zikists and
other adherents of Dr. Azikiwe with persons loyal to
himself. The development has been at the expense of
competing groups from Onitsha, Owerri, and Port Harcourt, although Port Harcourt is asserting its rights
increasingly and with mounting success. The Zikists seem
to have lost control of key positions and are therefore less
influential than when Dr. Azikiwe was Premier of the
Eastern Region. At the moment, their power potential is
latent but still considerable.

Major changes in patterns of influence that can tenta-
tively be discerned are the shift of power from the
governmental apparatus that was operated as a moderate
control mechanism by the colonial regime and by the
early self-government regime to an apparatus which re-
flects the progressive fusion of state, party, and society—
in other words, to an incipient "totalitarian" apparatus
(although this is still far removed from the German or
Russian models) and the expansion of the control mecha-

nism into all sectors of state and society, including traditional rule, education, private business, trading, and transportation.

Even where opposition elements occasionally succeed, with the support of religious, tribal, clan or other local forces temporarily galvanized over a given issue, in winning elections to the regional Parliament as Independents or as dissident NCNC representatives, they are as a rule effectively denied access to key control posts and hence deprived of sources of influence they can use to retain their positions, which of course are unsanctioned by the party. As autonomous sources of political influence, they are destined to political obliteration through attrition if not persecution.

In the Eastern Region, the NCNC controls the major channels of communication of relevance to the influence and control mechanism, hence the principal gateways to wealth and power and, therefore, the interest and attention of the public, which appears to be increasingly concerned with material objectives and which increasingly regards politics, which in the East means NCNC politics, as the surest road to wealth.

With regard to internal political communications, a few tentative observations can be made. It is in the nature of politics that the principals, that is, the elected officials, need to operate through utterly reliable, assuredly discreet channels of communication. Telephones, cable services, even the mails, are not deemed secure enough. Governmental messenger services are considered unreliable for a variety of reasons, one being that they may potentially be under the influence of political rivals. As a result, for some time to come, political influence will more likely than not be exercised through direct, personal contact. Public administration officials are bypassed, official channels and jurisdictional dividing lines ignored if neces-

sary. The scarcity of skilled assistants and confidential
secretaries and the tradition of personal communication,
as well as the illegal nature of some pressure plays and
the resultant threat of prosecution, especially at the local
level, further counsel recourse to personal and direct
communication between the influencer and the person
being influenced. Some ministers and lesser party leaders
have found it necessary to employ paid personal informers and agents. Similarly, persons seeking to reach
the key decision-makers prefer, if possible, direct, personal contact.

Because local government, by its constitutional frame of
reference, is concerned in one way or another with most
social, economic, cultural, and political activities in the
region, and because of its substantial patronage potential,
the NCNC takes special pains to assure itself of control
over that strategic branch of government. By direct and
indirect means, the party has effectively pervaded the
local government structure at key points. Equipped with
an organizational structure that parallels that of local
government, the party uses local government, among
other instrumentalities, to maintain control of the region.
Although nominally the Ministry of Local Government
constitutes the apex of this particular control structure,
the NCNC's Eastern Working Committee, the hierarchy of
the party chairmen and secretaries, and the party ap-
pointees to strategic boards and commissions provide
direction and guidance.

Thus political influence outside party channels is not
likely to gain momentum in the East. The party machinery is in a position to intercept, if not stifle, nonparty
attempts at influencing decision-makers who themselves
are conditioned to respond only to party directives. If
nonparty influence is brought to bear on the decision-

making machinery, it is only after it has been cleared with appropriate party authorities.

B. Traditional Rulers, Tribal "Spokesmen," and Voluntary Associations

Traditional rulers in the East are effectively controlled, and renascent tribal power and related influence groupings operating at cross-purposes with the government are being progressively contained. These groupings generate a great deal of political noise, publicly demanding greater recognition of their "sons" and more amenities for their tribal area, but as far as critical socio-economic issues are concerned, the traditional rulers, never having been an effective force in that part of Nigeria, are less influential now than at the time of independence. As a group and individually they lack the skills, the know-how, and the power increment to overcome determined resistance or pressure by party elements. Today they have been reduced to mere "service" groups at the party's disposal. Where tribal groups have eluded the reach of the NCNC, they are deprived nevertheless of access to the sources of power and influence and lose even the advantages of a "service group," which at least can count on rewards for its contributions to the party's electoral triumphs.

In general, it can be concluded that the chiefs and immediate tributaries are too keen on gaining a share of the regional wealth to alienate the fount of it all, namely the party. Being no more than government "licensed" functionaries, they, as well as other nonparty elements, know that the political web at the disposal of the NCNC is extensive enough in retaliation not only to deprive them of their official positions but also to close to them any outlet for economic gain in the private sector.

Tribal interest representation appears tribal in name only when it is brought to bear on the decision-making process. Its contents have undergone a metamorphosis, the catalyst being the tribal "spokesman." As the "spokesman" enters the mainstream of political influence, he becomes more and more concerned with his own personal interests, such as the attainment of income-producing public positions, or he represents in fact the interests of a commercial group, like the contractors, who conceal their private economic objectives behind appeals to tribal interests. This would suggest that some generalizations about the role of tribes in modern nation-building and related subjects may invite reconsideration.

Naturally, whoever seeks to exercise political influence derived from the vote-getting potential of a tribal grouping, or a clan, will cloak his argumentation in appeals to tribal values and interests.[7] However, as soon as a public position has been attained, the so-called tribal "spokesman," even the traditional ruler, begins to decry tribalism and localism as divisive, enervating, debilitating forces that must be discouraged in favor of a broader appeal to either regional or even national unity.

Data collected seem to indicate that within the Eastern regional context tribal support is fostered by political leaders primarily as a nest egg or a political insurance, to be drawn upon when needed for added strength in party councils, especially for the benefit of nominating committees.

Locally based, so-called tribal unions and other voluntary associations generally seem to be the closest approximation to organized pressure and interest groups in the Eastern Region, probably in all of Southern Nigeria.[8] Their main *raison d'être* appears to be generation of pressure on the regional and federal governments—and on migrated former residents of their respective communities —for financial contributions and political support of their claims for amenities, public construction programs, business and employment opportunities, scholarships, and so forth. Groups of that type appear to have greater internal cohesion and political endurance than may be said of most, if not all, trade unions, professional associations, and the like.[9] By all appearances, one should ascribe to these groups a certain influence potential. However, it seems that because of their demonstrated political strength party leaders eye these groups with profound suspicion, regarding them as actual or potential rivals for power and influence, and as threats to their own political survival. Consequently leaders of these groups frequently find themselves criticized, pilloried, and occasionally victimized by party-dominated local authorities, boards, or commissions.[10]

It appears that the influence potential of leaders of most of these groups is a direct function of either their identification with the interests of the local political party, the NCNC (in which case they are really auxiliaries of the party), or it is a function of family-, clan-, or township-derived identification with key persons in the influence and power structure in the region, i.e., within the NCNC high command or in the Cabinet. Interest groups of this type are most likely to achieve their objectives in the long run if their leaders are members of the NCNC. Leaders of local improvement leagues and town unions who are either politically unidentified or, worse, are identified with opposition groups, are likely to be politically impotent and destined for quick removal by their own followers.

There can be little doubt that improvement, welfare, tribal, and other locally oriented unions, leagues, and associations continue to reflect in their political argumentation certain tribal survival interests. However, the data collected would indicate that, at the moment at least, concern with economic and technological modernization

tends to eclipse tribal concern, partly because the latter
tends to be dysfunctional to the former. Welfare and
development societies can ill afford to indulge in tribal-
istic argumentation when seeking to attract investment by
outsiders.

C. The Ibo State Union (ISU)

Originally organized to promote Ibo ethnic interests,
the Ibo State Union became, partly as a result of the
struggle for power on the inter-regional plane, an auxiliary of the NCNC. Its importance varies inversely with the
relative strength of the Ibo group in a given constituency.
Where Ibos are in the minority, or are split for one
reason or another, the ISU serves to rally the members of
the tribe to the support of "their" party, the NCNC.
Because its vital survival interests manifestly hinge on the
political fortunes of the NCNC regime in the Eastern
Region, it cannot afford to weaken the hold of the NCNC
by public criticisms. It is therefore taken for granted by
the NCNC, a development which is causing some internal
disputes among the top leadership.

In terms of political influence, the Union's impact on the
authoritative decision-making structure is, in the circumstances, minimal. Whatever its interests, they must, to be
considered and acted upon at the highest levels, coincide
with the policies and political preferences of the party,
and, equally important, must then be formulated and
articulated by accepted party members. The sphere available to Ibo leaders for political maneuvers and influence
plays, aside from that explicitly allocated to it by the
party, is shrinking. It is accepted in the Eastern Region
that no matter how much the ISU may be ignored and
bypassed, it will eventually rally to the defense of the
NCNC when the need arises. Thus today the leadership of
the ISU cannot be viewed as independently powerful or
influential with regard to critical socio-economic issues.

Where ISU leaders appear to be powerful, they invariably are not so in their own right but merely as representatives or spokesmen of the party.

D. Organized Women

By far the greatest number of women active in public life are engaged in trading. The Party is therefore keen on assuring for itself the loyalty and support of their leaders, especially in the urban and municipal council areas, not only because they represent large numbers but also because their followers constitute the most important and effective link in the political communication system. This would suggest that leaders in this group are in a position to command significant bargaining power vis-à-vis the party and the government. However, data collected indicate that whatever influence potential may be attributed to these leaders is largely confined to matters related to trading, construction of market stalls, market fees, trading facilities and contracts, retail distribution, and the like. In exchange for recognition of at least the most pressing of their economic demands, leaders of this group, and most of the women generally, seem prepared to accept blindly the leadership of the party, loyally and even fiercely giving it their wholly uncritical support on all other issues, including women's rights and questions of integrity and honesty in public office, as well as on questions related to the survival of democratic institutions. The prime concern of leaders of this category seems to be accumulation of private wealth with the aid of the party.

E. Other Segments and Groups with Significant Influence Potential

1. *Contractors.* Politically, contractors (mainly those contracting with government agencies) appear to be increasingly influential. Government leaders consider them quite influential and regard them as "leaders of

thought."[11] Data collected indicate an increasingly active
role by large, medium, and petty contractors (contracts
below £1000 and over £100,000 were given as the upper
and lower limits of classification). Their principal sources
of influence in the large and medium categories are ability
to dispose of sizable capital funds and consequent close
relations to ministers and party leaders, and control over
large numbers of sub-contractors and employees, in some
cases on a regional scale. Contractors in the £100,000
range appear to constitute a significant source of revenue
for party or politicians or both. Many politicians seem to
regard them as "the geese that lay the golden eggs." Most
contractors seem to have some connection with the party,
as contributing "patron," as working committee member
or local chairman, as member of the House of Assembly,
or as an ordinary party member.

Contractors appear to be closely watched and regularly
contacted and consulted by party officials; the more
affluent ones by top leaders, the lesser ones by local
political leaders and officials. Petty contractors appear to
be in the forefront of local urban county, county, and
ward politics, constituting, at that level, a relatively active
pressure group.

2. *Male Traders, Traders' Associations*. Like the
women traders, these groups tend to follow the party in
power except where their own relatively narrow economic
interests are concerned. They seem to be only a shade
more critical of party performance on other issues than
the women. Their main concerns seem to be trade, trade
facilities, market fees and construction of stalls, and
taxes. Because of their isolation from similarly oriented
groups elsewhere in the region, and because of the low,
marginal income levels characteristic of their membership, their ability to enter into contests of power against

the government, at all levels, is extremely restricted. Their ability to conduct protracted strikes has been demonstrated to be rather low. The leadership of these groups is weak and it is doubtful that they can translate whatever control they may have over their followers into effective political influence at the various critical levels of decision-making. Unless galvanized into coordinated action by major, deep-seated grievances with mass appeal, these groups actually function in the form of relatively autonomous segments, strictly compartmentalized by the product they happen to sell.

When aroused, they seem to be capable of staging upsets in regional, but more likely in local elections. Thus, they appear to have been responsible, in Onitsha in 1961, for the loss by the NCNC of several seats in regional and local legislative bodies. In 1963, in Enugu, a combination of traders succeeded in staging a strike which was promptly called off without real settlement of the grievances when the party leadership began to apply pressure.[12]

3. *The Catholic Church.* Because of its dominant position in the Eastern Region's educational structure, the Catholic Church, especially its lay organizations, appears to command significant influence potential. However, its influence appears to be confined, in the main, to issues related to education. A substantial number of the social and political leaders in the Region are products of Catholic schools, and without the material and organizational assistance of the Catholic Church in the educational system, education in the Eastern Region would quickly encounter severe difficulties. This appears to be generally accepted among the authoritative decision-makers in the Region. Consequently, the Catholic hierarchy, operating rather discreetly at strategic points, and the Catholic lay

leaders, operating more openly and participating overtly
in party politics and election campaigns, can count on
sympathetic responses to their demands for concessions in
the general area of education. Occasionally the intense
jealousy affecting relations between Catholics and Protestants in the Region results in an essentially secular controversy assuming denominational proportions. To assure
themselves advantageous positions in the political power
structure in the Region and to reduce the influence of the
rival denominational group, Catholics and Protestants
agitate continuously for improved representation of their
particular faith in the regional Cabinet and in key positions within the administrative structure generally.
Teacher training, management of schools, universal primary education, state support for public schools, and
related controversies are always likely to precipitate intense rivalry between the major denominations.

II. WESTERN REGION[13]

The collapse in 1962 of the Action Group (AG) Government in the West, the Declaration of the Emergency in
May of that year, and the aftermath, have significantly
affected the patterns of political influence in the Western
Region. The creation of the Mid-West Region—carved out
of the old Western Region—further contributes, of course,
to these changes. It appears, however, that one characteristic of the influence pattern in the East, namely the
primacy of party politics and its corollary, extension of
party control into every conceivable sector of state and
society, is retained in the West, except that there it has
assumed pluralistic features. The division of power between the Western wing of the NCNC and the UPP has
introduced an element of dualism into some instrumentali-

ties of power and influence; where the AG still maintains its hold, a triple division has developed.[14]

A. The Political Parties.*

As in the East, the channels of political communication are reserved primarily to party politics and serve in the main to improve the office-holding and electoral chances of the political parties and of individual politicians. Since the Emergency in 1962, which demonstrated the ability of the federal coalition of the Northern People's Congress (NPC) and conservative NCNC politicians to inject itself into Western regional politics, political influence in the West has been largely a function of the ability of Western politicians to make themselves acceptable at the same time to the combination NPC–NCNC in the federal capital of Lagos and UPP–Western NCNC in the regional capital, Ibadan. The survey produced impressive evidence that numerous lines of political influence in the West run through Lagos. The once controlling Action Group now commands less influence, of course, but cannot be counted out because of its appeal to the extremely potent nationalism of the dominant tribe in the West, the Yorubas. Within the regional UPP–NCNC coalition, it appears at the time of writing to be the latter party which exercises greater and more widespread influence in the Region, partly because it seems to command greater strength at the grassroots. The apex of the power and influence structure in the West, aside from NPC or NCNC politi-

---

* In 1964, the Nigerian National Democratic Party (NNDP) was created from a fusion of the UPP and a portion of the Western wing of the NCNC. The remnants of both, the AG and the NCNC coalesced in the United Progressive Grand Alliance (UPGA). The NNDP, in turn, coalesced with the Northern People's Congress (NPC), and with several lesser parties, in the Nigerian National Alliance.

cians at the federal center, is presently occupied by
former Action Groupers and by leaders of the NCNC.

In general, the political parties of the West operate very
much as the NCNC does in the East. They draw on
essentially similar or identical socio-political sources of
influence, and employ essentially the same political
means. Where possible they seek to establish overt or
covert control over sources of revenue, including the
diversion of large sums of money, under one pretext or
another, into Party and/or private coffers.[15] They also
employ political patronage and the selective allocation of
public funds for improvements, amenities, dispensation of
scholarships, and the like. They avail themselves of the
ministerial powers assigned to their respective representatives under a coalition arrangement. Thus, the NCNC
exploits to the fullest the opportunities offered by the
Ministry of Local Government, which the NCNC's Western leader occupies. Like the Action Group before it, it
employs local government police, sanitary inspectors, contract controls, local service boards, threats of dissolution
of local councils, and the usual patronage opportunities
derived from the appointment powers allocated to the
Minister of Local Government.

There is ample evidence that in the tough and determined competition for political survival in the constituencies, with an eye to a future election to determine the
true succession to the fallen Action Group regime, some
leaders of both parties resort to rather aggressive measures, including the employment of informers, touts, and
even, where deemed necessary, physical victimization of
opposition elements.

Among party leaders, those who command relatively
firm support within a given constituency seem to be more
influential than those who lack that source of power and
influence. Among the more firmly established, those who

live in their constituency, preferably with deep family roots in the area, habitually maintaining an open door to all, distributing largesse, and in general continuously visible, seem to deserve a higher influence rating than those who fail to observe these fundamental requirements of Nigerian politics.

In the circumstances, few if any nonparty groups, among those inclined to resist the influence and control effect of the party leaders, will venture into the open. Those endowed with influence potential that might be regarded as alternative to that wielded by the present leaders seem to be awaiting the outcome of the intra-coalition struggle, of the sorting-out process precipitated by the fall of the Action Group, and of attempts to reconstitute Yoruba political cohesion. The victimization of former AG supporters that followed the seizure of power by the UPP–NCNC group has cast a pall over the Western Region political scene, especially over the palaces of those traditional rulers who had permitted themselves to become too closely identified with the Action Group. In view of the pressures applied by the AG while it was in power, it is difficult to blame traditional rulers for becoming identified with that party, but nevertheless they are being blamed by their subjects for misjudging the political situation.

The collapse of the AG regime and the resultant inter-party rivalry in the West appears to have brought about the replacement of the politician-businessman elite, created by the AG and highlighted in the report of the Coker Commission, by a new power elite made up primarily of party managers and, socio-economically speaking, "upstart" politicians.

B. Traditional Rulers

Traditional rulers, in their reticence, accentuated reserve, and move toward political nonalignment, reflect a

significantly altered influence pattern in the Region as
compared with the period preceding the changes in the
West. There can be little doubt, however, that with the
emergence of firm political party rule in the Region their
basic lack of power increment in the modern setting will
compel them once again to become associated with whatever political party emerges at the top.

It is widely held that traditional rulers still exercise
substantial influence at the local, tribal, and clan level.[16]
They still possess some discretionary powers which the
regional government leaves to them for convenience, if
for no other reason. However, data collected indicate that
traditional rulers, from the highest Obas to the village
chiefs, whenever possible carefully avoid contests of will
with the party-political leadership; their main aim appears to be to please the secular rulers, without involving
themselves too closely with any specific political party.
They hope to make themselves useful as communication
links between the government and the people, as arbitra-
tors and conciliators of local conflicts and disputes.
Meanwhile they keep an eye out for opportunities of
promotion, appointment to Cabinet or other high offices,
to courts, to commissions, or to honorific posts with
material emoluments attached.

To have value to their people, that is, to be effective in
the procurement of amenities for their tribal areas, Western traditional rulers, like those in the East, must as a
general rule develop close personal liaisons with the
ruling political party leaders. In the West, currently, it is
a measure of a traditional ruler's personal skill and acu-
men if he can maximize his utility to his people without
becoming too closely, possibly irretrievably, identified
with a political party which could be tomorrow's loser or
outcast.

Close questioning of various interest group leaders

revealed that aside from purely nominal, deferential references to the alleged influence wielded by traditional rulers, few, if any, were prepared to cite concrete illustrations of effective exercise of independent influence by traditional rulers in their major sphere of social responsibility. Many of these leaders, initially inclined to attribute significant influence potential to chiefs, seemed to be quite unimpressed with the power and prestige of these people once the interview established the absence of concrete substantiating evidence. Evidence obtained indicates that traditional rulers are given to claim credit for ideas and public measures that actually originated with public officials, usually local government personnel, and with the realization and implementation of which they had little if anything to do. Also, there is evidence that even ceremonious and dramatic invocation of traditional prestige in support of unpopular public policy proposals, such as the introduction of a tax system, cannot stave off defeat of a measure.[17]

Generally, the leaders of the political parties seem to delimit the zones of influence left to the traditional rulers and the latter are being reduced more and more to service elements, or transmission belts, for the political party or parties in power.

C. Summary Observations for the Western Region

1. *Pressure and Interest Groups.* The fragmentation of political power patterns as a result of the collapse of the Action Group regime has, theoretically at least, increased the opportunities for independent assertion of diverse group interests in the Western Region. The break-up of the AG political and financial empire has enhanced the relative influence potential of the several major non-Yoruba ethnic groups and sub-Yoruba groups (there being some doubt as to the true limits of the Yoruba nation).[18] The Egbas, Oyos, Ekitis, and Ijebus have now

improved opportunities to advance their claims for amenities and social and political recognition generally.[19] The same can be said of non-ethnic, functional pressure and interest groups. On the other hand, since all these groups have similar deficiencies of leadership, internal organizational strength, communications, and social orientation, they find it most difficult to resist successfully the range of counterpressures emanating from the political parties desperately searching for improved positions of power from which to overcome their rivals in the intra-regional and inter-regional power struggle.

Thus, what might appear to be independent pressure or interest groups (farmers' organizations, labor unions, drivers' unions, students' unions, women's organizations, traders' organizations and associations) may in reality, in terms of their political origin, direction, and behavior, more appropriately fall into the category of political party auxiliaries.[20]

Because of the predominance of illiterates and semiliterates on the executive bodies of the majority of tribal and other local associations, it is not too difficult for a well-trained, purposeful lawyer, teacher, or party official to direct any such association from outside. This appears to apply even to groups as potent as the Ogboni secret society in the West. On the other hand, evidence was obtained that indicates that groups such as the Ogbonis can still play a negative influence role on their own, i.e., they can obstruct, frustrate, and generally foment unrest.

It is also apparent that because political party connections are so essential to the attainment of group objectives, the tribal communication mechanism has *de facto* advanced the party leader, or more broadly, the party politician, as the tribal spokesman, replacing the traditional ruler as the principal articulator of group interests. The latter may still make the pilgrimage to the ministry but he should be under no illusion about the true nature of the influence channels his group must cultivate in order to obtain its share of the amenities, scholarships, and appointments. Several tribal groups, e.g., the Urhobos, the Binis, the Egbas, the Itsekirris, to mention but a few who came to attention, acknowledged reality and have invited politicians to take over the effective leadership of the group with regard to formulation of group goals and representations at the appropriate levels of governmental authority.

It can be generalized from the evidence obtained that the political parties appear to have taken over the appeal which groups like the Egbe Omo Oduduwa, the Ibo State Union, and similar organizations may have had not too long ago. The public, and the leaders in particular, have long realized that the fount of wealth and power are the political parties, and are therefore unwilling to entrust their interests to officials of moribund organizations. The attendance reports and the fact that few persons of note seem to attend meetings of tribal unions these days may be indicative of the waning influence of leaders from that segment, unless, as has been pointed out, these leaders also play a role in a ruling political party. At any rate, the tribal unions seem to be turning away from the traditional rulers as their principal spokesmen.

2. *Lines of Jurisdiction.* As in the East, lines of legal administrative jurisdiction seem to be observed only among members of the federal and regional parliaments, and even that is not too certain. There does not seem to be a rule of conduct concerning allocation of spheres of political influence which political leaders tend to honor in all respects. Thus it is entirely possible for a member of a legislature to attempt to create a base for himself or his party by entering the influence play in the district of a colleague by surreptitious means, e.g., promotion of arti-

ficial opposition through personal informers and representatives.

Similarly, anyone wishing to obtain the ear of a member of parliament, a minister, or a member of a city
council approaches his target directly—at home if he feels
so inclined.[21] As a result, there is within the influence
structure a great deal of up-and-down flow through face-
to-face contact. (One by-product of this is the remarkable
ability of the leaders to inform one of the whereabouts, at
any given moment, of most of their own immediate
colleagues and adversaries.)

3. *Regional and Local Government Officials.* Because of
the sheer volume of close contact dealings, public business
conducted in certain ministries, mainly the Ministry of
Local Government, and depending on the style of operation of the given minister, permanent secretaries, provincial secretaries, and local clerks, can under ideal conditions gather considerable power in their hands. Provided
the official in question understands how to avoid giving
the impression to his superior, or to political leaders
generally, that he is out either to embarrass or replace
them, a great deal of discretionary influence can be at the
disposal of a skillful person in that group. Conclusive
determination of influence potential in this group would
require more exhaustive analysis of the factors mentioned. For the time being, however, it may be stated that
because of the stakes at issue in the inter-party struggle,
at all levels, party leaders are most sensitive to public
officials who appear to compete with them for influence
and popularity, and the officials appear to be fully sensitive to these feelings. However, within the room left for
maneuver, public officials do exercise some quiet, un-
dramatic influence, especially where their political supe-
riors lack the requisite skills to understand what is going
on.

4. *Intellectuals and Professionals.* There is a tendency to attribute considerable influence potential to intellectuals and professionals, such as lawyers, teachers, and doctors. This may stem from the social prestige normally attached to members of this group. No doubt their skills and social prominence tend to enhance their political weight and, it would seem, should endow them with a certain ability to exert pressure successfully at government levels. Their ability to articulate public issues, and at times to have their views widely publicized in the press, should also, theoretically at least, lend weight to their opinions. But articulation, social prestige, reputation, etc., are a far cry from implementation. At any rate, evidence collected in the present survey tends to cast doubt upon the assumption that members of this group, as intellectuals or professionals and not in some other capacity, command appreciable influence at key decision-making levels. Their advice, if and when it is solicited, is not necessarily taken. By all indications, advice emanating from these circles appears to be suspect among leading politicians. The fact that numerous members of this group, especially teachers and lawyers, entertain political ambitions of their own tends to orient them toward compliance with the ruling power group and to discourage attempts to influence that may be misinterpreted by the politicians whom they wish to impress and whose support they may require.

It is possible that some sections of the public are inclined to be influenced by members of this group. Public agitation over the proposed Preventive Detention Act in 1963 may have been traceable in part to the nearly solid opposition to that measure among intellectuals and professionals. On the other hand, as pointed out elsewhere, Southern Nigerian politicians were themselves in profound disagreement about the correct timing of such a step and may themselves have been instrumental in its abortion.

The weight of evidence collected would indicate that intellectuals and professionals, as such, seem to be as much under the sway of the wielders of political control power as any other group; now, following the "treason" convictions of members of the Action Group in September 1963, and amidst increasing pressure on the university faculties to conform, this group, in the aggregate, may be more cowed than before.

As a matter of exercising influence directly within the authoritative decision-making context, this group appears to have influence only where the principal wielder of decision-making power has reason to believe that a given communication or piece of advice from a doctor, teacher, or lawyer is not designed to expose him to public ridicule, or, more important, is not designed to lead to his removal from office. Political affiliation on the intellectual's or professional's part tends to reduce his influence potential as an intellectual or professional. Politicians seem to be suspicious of advice tendered by professional men and women, even of their own party, if they have reason to believe that the objective is their ultimate removal from office. One respondent, replying to an unscheduled spot question: "Do you find literates reliable in your party work?" said typically, "I can use literates when they are not eager to stand for the House or something like that."[22]

Lawyers as such, and as a group, have little influence potential. The Nigerian Bar Association, for instance, appears to be paralyzed on controversial issues because of the divergent interests of its membership, a good proportion of whom are beholden to the regional government and to political parties through positions as legal advisers, positions which bring substantial retainer fees in many instances but which tend not to be taken too seriously by the political leaders. Expectations of court appointments and of political careers, government briefs, and the like, tend to keep lawyers and their associations well in line. Lawyers do exercise effective political influence mainly where they perform not as lawyers but as party leaders or officials. In that capacity they do, of course, play a most prominent part.

5. *Businessmen.* Businessmen, particularly contractors, seem too dependent upon the regional government to exercise any appreciable influence, in the critical context here examined. It is within the power of a minister, if backed by the Cabinet, including the Premier, to bring a politically undesirable businessman close to ruin. As in the East, numerous instrumentalities are available to the politician to reward cooperation and to punish non-cooperation. Some contractors appear to wield some influence through holds over ministers developed as a result of mutually satisfactory arrangements, although it is difficult to determine who is influencing whom between the contractor and a given minister.

III. SOME TENTATIVE CONCLUDING OBSERVATIONS

It appears that although Southern Nigeria has its share of organized and spontaneous *ad hoc* interest and pressure groups, whose main *raison d'être* is to attempt to influence key decision-makers at the several levels of government, few if any of these groups command the means and are capable of generating sufficient pressure to assure satisfaction of their demands unless these demands are closely aligned with the political interests and purposes of the ruling political parties. Stated differently, it would appear that with the exception of certain dramatic occurrences which stir wide circles of the public to action so that public opinion makes itself felt independently, political parties permeate all social and economic activities in the Regions, and considerations of a party-political nature seem to govern the behavior of most if not all of the significant nonparty groups. With regard to the influence structure in Southern Nigeria this can be interpreted to mean that the flow of influence from the source of a given interest or idea to its implementation by decision-makers is largely a function of the political party machinery. Where the party leadership is responsive to influence from below or outside the party, mainly for electoral purposes, the flow may be both upward and downward. Where the party is relatively or absolutely secure in its position of power, in the East more than the West or Mid-West, the flow is likely to be mainly downward, following with few exceptions the outlines of the party hierarchy. Influence upon decision-makers then becomes largely a matter of translating directives reflecting party goals and serving party purposes into legislative or administrative action. In such circumstances, groups originally organized to exercise influence independently on behalf of certain social or economic causes or claims are transformed into dependent groups serving the dominant political party as an additional instrument of propaganda or party auxiliary. This pattern does not, of course, rule out selective political party responsiveness to matters of public interest. It merely means that such interests are largely subordinated and shaped by the party leadership to conform with the party's goals and purposes. Exceptions appear to be such instances as occurred in the summer of 1963 when the regional premiers contemplated legislation to enable the regional governments to detain persons suspected of treasonable activities. The measure had to be postponed; it is probable that postponement was aided by spontaneous widespread public opposition. It is also possible that substantial disagreement among the Nigerian leaders concerning the timing for such a controversial measure forced postponement. At any rate, the data collected in this survey would indicate that, as a rule, public opinion does not become aroused so easily in Southern Nigeria; on the contrary, it appears to have a very high tolerance threshold with regard to absence or loss of freedoms.

Only a few groups seem to have been able to generate sufficient power to assert themselves against the party leadership. This appears to have been a function primarily of organizational weakness of the party in certain areas and of the control, on the part of given interest groups, of a substantial share of economic or social power. Thus, Catholic religious organizations were able to defeat an attempt to restrict the scope of parochial schools through Universal Primary Education, and on occasion they have elected candidates sympathetic to their cause over the opposition of the NCNC hierarchy. Similarly, some organizations of traders, both men and women, have occasionally succeeded in wresting concessions from governmental authorities in defiance of the party's will. Given a relatively competitive electoral situation, town unions, improvement leagues, welfare organizations, and clan associations have sometimes been able to record modest successes in achieving some of their goals, e.g., installation of water pipes, construction of a hospital, a road-building program, a new government-controlled plant.

Undoubtedly, tribes, and traditional rulers in particular, are still playing significant roles in the context of political influence. Traditional rulers certainly must be assumed to continue to play significant roles in the more nebulous processes which generate public opinion and social influences of one kind or another. Their advice is

in all probability still being accepted by substantial por-
tions of the illiterate public in the every-day phases of
traditional life and by illiterate voters, especially in rural
and municipal elections.

However, for present purposes it should be noted that
traditional rulers have steadily lost independent political
power to secular leaders, probably ever since introduction
of self-government in the early 1950's. By all evidence
obtained in the present survey, they have now been reduced, with a few notable exceptions, to mere instrumentalities of the political rulers, especially the political
party leadership. What appears to be independent role-
playing, in elections for example, may in actuality be no
more than an acting out of party directives couched,
where appropriate, in tribalist terminology. Both the
chiefs and the party leaders are well aware of the relative
ease with which a traditional ruler can be deposed in
present-day Nigeria. Chiefs adjust their behavior accordingly.

In the East, where the principal source of political
influence, the NCNC, enjoys a virtual monopoly of power,
it can wield influence to the exclusion of other groups to
the point of nearly "total" control, with the usual modifications of the term "total" which one should apply in the
African context. Although factions do of course operate
within the Region and within the party itself, the power
potential in the hands of the party leadership appears to
be sufficient to overcome all but the most persistent
opposition. Where deemed essential to party purposes,
even die-hard opposition can be eliminated or at least
overcome. At any rate, the party can and does interfere
with the free exercise of influence by nonparty groups
upon decision-makers at the several levels of government.

In the West, and even more so in the still comparatively
wide-open Mid-West, where several parties still must

compete for public support, factions and oppositional groupings generally should be expected to be able to exert influence upon authoritative decision-makers, and the governing political parties should be relatively responsive to claims and demands advanced by various independent groupings. Here too, however, the lack of cohesiveness and sustaining power characteristic of interest and influence groups in developing societies hampers their effectiveness and enables the ruling political parties effectively to stifle, or at least sidetrack, claims and demands deemed not in line with party policy or with the aims of the governing politicians.

Within the major political parties, the NCNC and the UPP–AG, patterns of influence have emerged that indicate the following characteristics. In the East, the apex of the NCNC power structure—the point where influence to be most effective would have to be applied—is occupied without effective challenge from anywhere by the manipulators of the statutory and political instrumentalities which are crucial in the allocation of resources.

In the West, control of the key power instrumentalities is contested between the leaders of the NCNC and NPC–federal coalition, and by the "upstarts" in the NCNC and the UPP who inherited power in the Western Region as a result of the collapse of the Action Group system. Some leaders of the Western coalition appear eager to disengage themselves from Lagos, partly because of all-Yoruba sentiments now spreading through the Region, partly because of their own desire to establish effective Western Region control over the sources of wealth and all that this implies.*

Of relevance to the relative openness of the channels of communication for political influence is the fact that in

---

* In 1965, prior to the Western Regional election, several leaders of the Western wing of the NCNC joined the ruling NNDP.

the East, and possibly everywhere in Nigeria, a certain
stiffening in the attitude of the ruling political party
elements towards their actual and potential adversaries
seems to have taken place. As a result, rational dialogue
between government and opposition and between government and private interests is becoming ever more difficult.
Government by persuasion gives way to government by
coercion. On the other hand, it seems to be in accordance
with tradition that personal relations between contending
forces are not necessarily disrupted. Thus, in the West,
certain characteristics of Austrian politics (with certain
modifications, of course) are discernible. In Austria from
1918 to 1955 Fascists, Socialists, National Socialists,
Nationalists, and Liberals knew each other personally,
were engaged in continuous dialogue with each other,
even assisted each other when one group was being
incarcerated by another. In Western Nigeria, leaders of
the fallen Action Group (those at liberty, that is), and
leaders of the NCNC and the UPP appear to maintain
personal contact throughout what, by public manifesta-
tions, appear to be bitter political contests. The sense of
"national" pride growing among the Yoruba may be a
contributing factor in this development.

Whatever the personal relations, however, publicly the
channels of communication in Southern Nigeria do not at
present appear to be open enough to encourage the free
flow of ideas and interests and the free exercise of varied
political influences in competition or even in conflict with
ruling political parties. The generation of ideas outside
regular party channels seems to be resented by party
leaders and is generally discouraged.[23]

Channels of communication linking the relatively un-
educated, untrained, or educated but anti-intellectual
political party leadership to the most knowledgeable, educated, highly trained members of the Nigerian intelli-

gentsia, including the professions, do not appear to be as open as is commonly assumed. Ideas entertained by the latter are not necessarily being communicated effectively to the former. But within certain lower level groups, intellectuals do appear to play leading roles.

The major share of the time devoted to public affairs by the political party leaders, including members of the several legislative bodies, appears to be allocated to contact with constituents, or petitioners in general; this appears to be more true of the politically competitive West than of the East. Ideological considerations, related either to internal or external questions, do not appear to play a significant part in the political influence structure, notwithstanding the fact that public pronouncements are frequently couched in ideological terms. Consultations with constituents appear to center on matters related to the education of the young, including the procurement of scholarships, the settlement of domestic disputes, employment questions, procurement of loans for trade and construction, political career advice, taxes, and defense against political victimization, in that order of frequency.

Previous research, admittedly considerably less systematic and methodically less well structured than the present survey, had led to the conclusion that control over the means of production and allocation of wealth was crucial in the political influence structure. Accordingly it was assumed that certain leaders of business, finance, and industry, both indigenous and expatriate, occupied key positions in the influence structure. It was noted, however, that indigenous leaders frequently had gained access to wealth through acquisition of political power, largely derived from association with nationalist movements and drives.[24] Present research indicates that both expatriate and nonparty indigenous business interests have experienced a marked decline in power and influence since independence, and that indigenous political leaders, basing their power primarily on party association, are now dominating business, finance, and industry as well.

Are Political Considerations More Important in Southern Nigeria than Nonpolitical Ones?

The questions asked in the present survey were sufficiently broad to have produced evidence that, within the authoritative decision-making influence structure, nonpolitical considerations, e.g., purely technical, economic, cultural, spiritual, or ideological, exceed political ones in intensity and frequency if such had been the case. Instead, the data collected warrant the conclusion that political considerations, and among those, party-political ones, overshadow all other types. Beyond that, such critical functions as leadership recruitment appear to be entirely under the sway of party politics, not only in the political parties and in public agencies, but in social, cultural (including lay-clerical), ecomonic, and professional groups as well.

The principal channels of communication of relevance to the exercise of influence over the outcome of critical socio-economic issues appear to be firmly in the control of political party leaders whose major concerns are management of political power, retention of office and continuous acquisition of additional means of power and influence. Of distinct benefit to the public interest, of course, is the evident preoccupation of the ruling elite in Southern Nigeria with the discovery of public issues the espousal of which contains the promise of political reward. Among those, the provision to constituents of amenities looms most prominently at the present time, possibly with adverse effects on the federal and regional economic development plans.[25]

The degree of party-political dominance over all phases of public life is of course greatest in the Eastern Region, where at the time of writing the NCNC enjoyed a virtual monopoly of power. In such circumstances, none of the competing social and political forces, large or small, can hope to have its views reflected in the authoritative decision-making structure except by permission and authorization of the party. To be taken into account in this respect is the nearly total control by the party of all principal channels of communication, of all significant control points in the regional economy, and thereby of the sources of support and sustenance of all actual or potential competitors. If, under these conditions, nonpolitical interests want to make themselves felt in the influence structure, they will be able to do so only in terms acceptable to the jealous political party organization.

In the West, and the Mid-West for some time to come, while coalitions govern in a relatively open setting, some room is left for competition and rivalry, hence for injection of some nonpolitical considerations into the primary socio-economic influence stream. Stated differently, political parties in such a setting are more permissive, thus leaving room for nonpolitical interests to unfold and to make themselves felt at critical levels. But even in the Western Region, the primacy of politics suggests itself because no matter which of several ruling groups one may consider, one deals with forces based on political power, operated along political lines, inclined to give priority to political considerations, manipulating political influence instrumentalities, i.e., ministries, local councils, courts, and manipulating them primarily with a view to achievement of undisputed monopolistic political power and influence. Since even in the West all major instrumentalities of acquisition of wealth are in control of party leaders operating through regional ministries, or even federal ones, the purely nonpolitical force has little choice but to submit to the primacy of politics. Data collected tend to bear out that conclusion rather convincingly.

It appears that proposals, public policy or private, which require some form of authoritative decision-making by elected officials, at this point in time, are tested for their political survival value by these officials and are translated into action only if the test proves positive.

3

MASS PARTY
REGIMES IN AFRICA[1]

CLEMENT HENRY MOORE

Definition

Regimes depending upon an organized mass party are hardly new to the world. At the height of their power the Jacobins ran a rudimentary single-party regime in which the local clubs intervened—admittedly in unsystematic fashion—in the operations of the state administration.[2] In the context of more recent revolutions, apart from the obvious Fascist and Communist examples, Turkey and Mexico developed one-party regimes. So also did Egypt.

However, the mass party regimes established in Africa since Tunisian independence (March 20, 1956) ought to be distinguished even from their closest counterparts, in Turkey and Mexico, both of which depended initially upon military strong men. Only gradually (in the Mexican case, after many succession crises) was the original military basis of power firmly subordinated to a civil authority. In Africa, on the other hand, the political parties generally performed their national revolutions with little use of organized violence. In only one case to

date, that of Algeria, did a single-party regime emerge in
which the military or para-military forces were not
clearly subordinated to the party. (Of course, this did not
preclude military coups *after* independence, as in Togo.)
The Algerian FLN before independence, however, was
primarily a military organization rather than a political
party.

The new regimes might appear to resemble more closely
that of the Egyptian Wafd before World War II. However, the Wafd, though occasionally able to mobilize the
crowds in massive demonstrations, lacked the organization of the newer mass parties. Representing an indigenous landed class, the party was content to rule through
the traditional village headman, however much its leading
orators could sometimes empathize with the people. Eventually the party split when, too late, it tried to enlist the
support of the urban proletariat.[3]

The Wafd's failure to provide independent Egypt with
effective leadership in the 1930's is a practical if negative
reason for emphasizing in independent Africa today the
analytical distinction between regimes fostered and sustained by a single mass party and those based upon a
"patron" or "elite" party.[4] The former, at least before
they achieved power, aspired to carry out a social revolution as well as a political transfer of power. Thus their
leaders were recruited on the basis of political commit-
ment rather than social status. Membership and advance
within the party were open to all adults. In place of
decaying traditional structures of society, the new mass
parties installed modern cells or branches modeled on
those of the Communist or Socialist parties of the metropole. Local elections inside the party were relatively
democratic, and usually relations between the local and
national levels were maintained by regional federations
that were also democratically elected. The rhythm of

party activity was intense, and party discipline was the
norm that with varying degrees of effectiveness replaced
other sources of legitimacy. In Sigmund Neumann's
terms, the new mass party, like its parliamentary democratic counterpart in Western Europe, could truly be
called a "party of integration" rather than a "party of
representation."[5] In contrast, the patron parties relied
upon an existing social elite—traditional chiefs and head-
men, but also sometimes the more modern but conservative leaders in the colonial society—to serve as intermedi-
aries for the people.

Unfortunately, however, the theoretical distinction between mass and patron parties is sometimes difficult to
draw in practice. Depending upon the particular social
structure and level of political development, it may sometimes happen that the "patrons" can be democratically
elected and will develop a mass party organization to
modernize the basis of their popularity. Conversely, a
new, popularly recruited political elite may become at
least as closed, conservative, and organizationally inactive
as the patrons of more traditional societies. In the Ivory
Coast, for instance, the PDCI (Parti Démocratique de la
Côte d'Ivoire), an effective mass party in the late 1940's,
was allowed to atrophy simply because an active apparatus was not needed; its popular leader's position was
secure, and relations with France were harmonious after
the repression of 1949–50. Elsewhere conflict with the
colonial power often lasted until, and even after, independence, so that an apparatus for mass mobilization and
agitation continued to be needed. In the Northern Region
of Nigeria, on the other hand, the NPC (Northern
Peoples' Congress) leaders may feel compelled to transform their party, a classic example of the "patron" type,
into a more modern structure adequate for advancing and
containing social revolution.

The distinction between the two types of party also raises a theoretical issue that is important in the African setting. How is the mass party to achieve its mission of social integration—by totally uprooting and supplanting older intermediary bodies or by decisively influencing the latter's style of participation in the new society? Under the first formula the PDCI would never have qualified as a mass party; under the second, more flexible formula it would seem even today to qualify as one, though its local subcommittees are organized along ethnic rather than strictly geographic lines. It remains an open question whether the party's toleration of ethnicity (to be sure, out of weakness and inertia rather than for reasons the democratic pluralist might give) will hinder rather than serve national integration over the long run.[6] Moreover, data are not yet available for estimating the role ethnic arithmetic may play in the internal local politics of other, ostensibly more integrated mass parties.

Despite problems of both an empirical and theoretical nature, however, the distinction between mass and patron parties serves roughly to delimit our field of inquiry. We are concerned here with mass party regimes, the most clear-cut examples of which are to be found in Ghana, Guinea, the Ivory Coast, Mali, Nyasaland, Senegal, Tanganyika, and Tunisia. The parties vary in their effectiveness, but all of them lead much more than the purely formal existence characteristic of patron parties. Perhaps the most effective are the PDG (Parti Démocratique de Guinée) of Guinea, the Union Soudanaise of Mali, and the Neo-Destour of Tunisia—in terms both of their organizational activity and their historic significance as symbols of national unity and purpose. (In the latter respect the Neo-Destour, founded in 1934 and maintaining a continuous leadership, must probably be ranked first.)

These new regimes have little in common with totalitarian single-party regimes, though, as with those of the patron variety, the lines of demarcation may be blurred in practice. The African regimes are not totalitarian at present simply because they are unable to intervene in the lives of their citizens (despite Mali's *Brigades de Vigilance*) in the all-embracing manner which the term "totalitarianism" suggests. More specifically, these regimes do not fulfill three of the six characteristics one may ascribe to totalitarian dictatorships.[7] None yet has a "system of terroristic police control" or a "central control and direction of the entire economy," nor, more significantly, does any have an official totalitarian ideology— despite a glib use, often, of revolutionary imagery.[8] Clichés torn out of the context of metropolitan politics cannot alone provide a "chiliastic claim," when once independence has been achieved and the "vestiges of colonialism" have been removed. It is probably to alienated groups within the new societies that one must look for new potentially total ideologies. Without an ideological justification, it seems unlikely that the present regimes will exercise police repression beyond the pragmatic limits needed for staying in power.[9]

Indeed, it is the absence of an authentically revolutionary ideology after independence that perhaps accounts for their characterization as "extinct nationalist mass-movement regimes."[10] Their "extinct" quality, however, points up the weakness of Tucker's own comparative analysis of "movement-regimes," in which he presents three traits supposedly common to Communist, Fascist, and nationalist single-party regimes. He maintains that all share, in addition to a *mass* movement, a Leninist *party* and certain *revolutionary* characteristics—notably an enemy, either foreign or treated as foreign, and an ideology serving as an organizing instrument. But actually, in the first place, the African mass parties, unlike the

Leninist vanguard or Nazi elite, are open to everyone, or almost everyone, though admittedly not always on a voluntary basis. Second, the Leninist conception of the relations between party and state applies to some but not to all of the new African regimes (to Guinea and Mali, for instance, but *not* to Tunisia).

Third, it is precisely the loss of revolutionary momentum that accounts for these regimes—as soon as they are regimes, no longer opposition parties—becoming "extinct." Not even Guinea, after the honeymoon of independence, can afford to treat the ex-colonial power as an enemy. Ideology, the trappings of which are more developed in Guinea than anywhere else, seems to serve less as an organizing principle than as half-assimilated rhetoric. Often, as in Tunisia, communication is most effective when it consists of popular homilies expressing concrete, limited objectives. A concrete revolutionary ideology—a coherent system of ideas expressing a social vision and a means of attaining it in the vocabulary of the indigenous culture—must probably await a greater degree of cultural identity (or conflict), more political mobilization, and greater social differentiation than is presently to be found in any of the African mass party states.[11] The truth is that the mass parties, once independence has been completely won, no longer confront a revolutionary situation. They no longer have the tension of conflict with the colonial power to sustain their revolutionary zeal. To become a regime means primarily to consolidate power and perhaps to fan the embers of the revolutionary flame in pursuit of pan-Africanism while expending their energy on the mundane tasks of economic development—a sort of precondition for future revolution.[12]

It seems more prudent, then, to conclude that these new African regimes are *sui generis,* even though in a tautological sense they resemble other regimes ruled by a single party. Briefly, the African regimes under discussion share a few distinctive traits: the party is a mass rather than patron party: open to almost all nationals, it has a well-articulated and active structure that sustains a mass following and aims at integrating the society while providing political leadership; it arose in response to a colonial situation; it "struggled"—though sometimes only symbolically—against "colonialism" and "won" independence; and it is the preponderant party after independence, exercising a virtual monopoly of power, though weak opposition parties may persist.[13]

Tasks

Before further elaborating our model of the mass party regime, it seems useful, if the model is to be dynamic, to describe the problem these regimes confront and thus suggest the tasks that they ought to perform.[14] Since one-party systems are controversial, it is best to be explicit. Mass party regimes are attractive to many Africans and sympathetic Western observers because they appear to offer emerging nations a politics that is relatively stable and conducive to rapid economic development. Since classic parliamentary democracy has generally failed in non-Western countries, the regime of the single party may in fact be the only alternative to some other more fragile form of authoritarian rule, usually of the military, in most of these countries.

The hope of the single mass party is that it may provide effective leadership for tackling the gigantic problems of modernization while fostering the development of representative institutions. Obviously, a regime that is stable and confident of mass support stands a better chance of launching social and economic reforms. Leaders who are not threatened by the demagogy of a rival party may be better able to concentrate on their domestic problems and make rational decisions that are unpopular but necessary for development. With the support of a well-organized party, they may be able to avoid the pitfalls of excessive nationalism and preoccupation with foreign policy. For, unlike the leaders of more fragile regimes, they will have less need to assert their nationhood in search of popular applause and may be better able to explain practical policies and acquire enlightened support. The popular party will already serve as a focus for national identity, and its leaders may be able to channel the mass enthusiasm for independence into the constructive tasks of development. If the regime can maintain its popularity and inspire social and economic reforms in an atmosphere of consensus, it will not be precluding the development of a democratic process even though it is based upon a single party.

Such at least is what one might hope of a mass party regime. What specifically does such a hope entail, if it is to have any factual basis? There would be a number of tasks that the party (along with related organizations, such as youth groups and trade unions) would have to perform. It would have to be making effective, rational decisions after independence. These would include consolidating the new state as well as launching whatever reforms were needed for development. Furthermore, once consolidated in power, the single party would have to continue to recruit a political elite, educate the people politically, represent them, and integrate them into the new nation. These four tasks, suitably defined, may serve as paradigms of party activity in mass party regimes that are already going concerns.

In conjunction with the government, the party and its auxiliary organizations (trade union, youth, student, women's) are the sole means of political recruitment. In industrial societies there are usually other means of access to power or influence, such as the business corporation, the army, the university, and the plethora of interest groups and other independent associations. But in the single-party regime few autonomous organizations are allowed to serve such a purpose even when they have a life of their own. Questions immediately arise: Is access to influence and power relatively open within the party regime? Are the leaders open to suggestions from below? Does the regime attract the participation of the political animals of the society?[15]

A general facet of political education is "political socialization"—the inculcation of political culture at all levels of the society. In industrial societies, many groups perform such a function, but in transitional societies, where new political styles and values are being introduced, the work falls largely upon the single party. Politics acquires increasing scope, as the new values may comprise a whole new way of life involved in the process of modernization. The party—and more especially the leader—must display an extraordinary aptitude for manipulating the symbols of the old society and devising new ones. The political process itself—the play, the aura of progress which it may exude—may be the prime source of new rituals, and hence often of symbols through which values can be communicated. An aspect of this education, the ritual part, is what some have called "mass mobilization"—drumming up mass enthusiasm for goals like independence or economic development. Education may also be of a more specific nature, explaining a government project or policy to the people where their cooperation is needed.

Representation and integration are two somewhat incompatible functions. Where integration needs to be emphasized, representation is apt to be minimized, yet, so far as integration is achieved and results in consensus, more genuine representation is possible. In other words, a society enjoying a greater amount of cohesion and consensus should be able to afford more democratic practices. The means of engineering the cohesion, however, may impede the development of representative processes. Yet —and here is a further dilemma for any modernizing regime—artificial integration, by demanding ritual performance without providing new meaningful symbols, may prove to hinder rather than help modernization. And without two-way communication, that is, some form of representation, the new symbols are apt to be stillborn.

Integration is an especially acute problem in transitional societies, and the single party is usually the prime instrument. The process may be observed at the national level among the elite, at the local level of village or tribal faction, and in the interrelation between the two levels in the political process. Nation-building is indeed such a basic problem in new states that it has sometimes been virtually identified with the broader problem of modernization.[16] Briefly, a single party is performing the task of integration when it induces cohesion and consensus on basic national values and objectives among the elite, transmits the consensus to the people, and provides new local structures to replace dying ones.[17] The important question, of course, is how the party goes about performing this triple function. Are the means compatible with the party's representative role?

Representation is the most controversial task to assign the single party. Those prejudiced against one-party regimes doubt that a monopolistic party is able in any significant sense to fulfill a representative role. Others who consider democracy to be a utopian dream for underdeveloped countries may doubt the relevance of the issue.[18] Apologists for the mass party regime, on the other hand, are apt to argue that these parties (or at least their party) practice internal democracy and represent "all the people." Often the apologists and the detractors are arguing at cross purposes because they attach different meanings to representation and "democracy."

The issue is an important one which ought not to be dismissed with the utopian's or pessimist's respective assumptions that democracy is either bound to develop or is only possible in economically advanced countries.[19] Representative institutions may perhaps develop over time and reflect other social transformations, but they certainly do not "take off" with economic growth—a crash landing is more likely under the strains of industrialization. Unless there is some attempt at democratic rule during the early stages of modernization, the prospect for democracy would seem even more remote for subsequent stages. Conversely, modest efforts at democratic rule might nurture representative traditions.

Moreover, the party's representative role has an important bearing on the outcome of its other activities. If recruitment is to remain effective after independence, a measure of internal party democracy would seem essential. If political education is profoundly to transform the values of the society and adapt them to the demands of modernization, dialogue between educators and the audience cannot be a one-way street. If the party is really to integrate the nation, the new consensus must be genuine and lasting, resting on persuasion and thoughtful participation, not repression or ritual applause.

Of course, there is a sense in which a mass party may be "representative" by virtue solely of an aspect of its integrative activity. The party—and especially its leader—that incarnates the nation, focuses its loyalties, manipulates its symbols, provides its sense of identity, and

wins free elections by overwhelming majorities quite
clearly represents the people. But even the elections are
simply a ritual of participation, a diffuse gesture, a
symbol of belonging to the nation for the new mass of
voters. Politics, if it consists only of voting, parades,
fiery speeches, and flag-waving, remains a mere spectacle
—a spectacle, however, that superficially furthers national
integration.

Direct mass representation is possibly a useful device in
politically backward countries for eliciting some feeling
of participation in the political process. Universal
suffrage, however, would hardly appear to be a useful
restraint upon government when the electoral outcome is
never in doubt.[20] In most underdeveloped countries, too,
the idea of direct mass representation—one man, one vote
—is simply an indiscriminate adaptation of the political
style of advanced countries. Rarely does the electorate
have any clear understanding of national issues, even if
there happen to be two or more parties effectively competing for votes. Mass representation in a single-party system can sometimes be pernicious as well as irrelevant—
when, for instance, party manipulators can crush legitimate interest groups or smother new ideas of the modern
elite in the name of a mathematical mass majority. For
the sake of national integration, too, electoral laws for
parliamentary elections are designed to minimize contact
between the deputy and his constituency[21] and maximize
control by the party machine over the deputies.

Another seemingly more relevant theory is that of
indirect representation, through interest groups. Everybody in the society, it might be argued, has concrete
material interests that some group or groups may effectively represent even if all its members do not understand
the national issues at stake. Trade unions represent the
objective interest of the proletariat, and business, youth,

student, farmers' and women's organizations similarly represent their constituencies. Theoretically, in a well-organized mass party regime, everybody in the society may be represented by one of the party's auxiliary organizations, even if he is not an actual dues-paying member. Policy, then, may be hashed out among the various groups within the party framework.

The interest theory usually assumes, however, that everybody has some objectively determinable material interest and that somehow the leaders of the interest groups will loyally represent their respective interests. Actually these groups are relatively weak in underdeveloped countries, where professional specialization has not progressed as in industrial societies. Though the mass parties encouraged a remarkable proliferation of voluntary organizations even before independence, these auxiliaries in all cases were substantially weakened a few years after independence by being brought under the fuller control of the party.[22] A more general interest theory might include "natural" traditional groupings, but mass parties, combating "tribalism," displace the old structures and can at best replace them with new ones (party branches) which use some of the old symbols and styles in a broader context.

Modern professional or economic interests are irrelevant to the average citizen, though he may be inspired with patriotism or concerned with local issues. Even among the modern elite, concern with national politics usually outweighs any interest or feeling of identification with an economic or professional grouping. The possibilities of indirect interest representation, then (at least in the narrow sense of the term "interest," which gives it conceptual clarity), seem largely circumscribed in transitional societies. Indeed, an exclusive reliance upon indirect representation would also be pernicious if it justified interest groups, representing only a small, modern sector of the society, in monopolizing national politics to the detriment of less politically astute masses or at the expense of autonomous, educated citizens whose potential contribution is to enlighten opinion rather than to swell organizations.

Between the extreme abuses of mass and interest representation lies a range of possibilities perhaps better understood in practice than in theory. The problem of representation is peculiarly complex in heterogeneous underdeveloped societies. At the local level direct representation is possible whereby the people choose their village leaders. At the national level a measure of indirect representation may be practiced. Specialized groups, such as workers in trade unions, may actually succeed through their organizations in exercising some influence upon national politics, at least upon policies of special concern if not in the selection of national leaders.[23] It is among the country's educated elite that difficulties are apt to arise. If this elite is not in fact cohesive and does not share in a national consensus, the party is hardly likely to provide it with adequate channels to express itself, much less to select its leaders or to present alternative leadership. Faithful to the mission of integration, the party may not hesitate to suppress dissident newspapers, lock up political nonconformists, and generally trample upon the civil liberties it so ardently defended in the colonial era.

Dynamics

By definition all mass party regimes share comparable ideologies, structures, and historical origins. At the same time, if the above analysis is correct, they confront similar problems. Is it possible, then, to discern a common pattern in the evolution of these regimes? Is it possible, moreover, to explain differences—the degree, for instance, to which a regime may concentrate on its task of integration at the expense of representation—in light of ideological, structural, or historical variations?

To answer the latter question first, historical analysis may provide a key for explaining both ideological and structural variations and differences in subsequent patterns of development. The mass party always originates in a colonial situation, but these situations vary in "intensity." Intensity may be measured by such indices as duration of foreign rule, "direct" as contrasted with "indirect" rule, extent of economic development, spread of modern education, and number of colonial settlers. Qualitatively an intensive colonial situation involves a breakdown of the traditional structures sufficient to render the patron-type party obsolete and a colonial conflict sufficiently drawn out to require the nationalists to mobilize mass support. The prerequisite of any mass party regime, then, is a relatively intensive colonial situation.

An especially intensive kind of colonial situation stimulated what might be called a "colonial dialectic"[24] in Tunisia and, to a lesser extent, in Senegal and Ghana. Schematically, the full play of the dialectic may be seen in a succession of three "moments," or phases, reflecting three distinctive attitudes of the colonized elite toward the colonizer. The first moment, after the Western conquest, is one of admiration and awe. In a state of shock, the conquered elite tries to imitate the victor—by copying Western appearances and sending its children to European schools. Any pre-colonial feelings of a social identity seem obliterated; like the Hegelian slave, the society's foundations "quake within." Sheer negativity—uprooted consciousness shaken into self-consciousness—is hence the

other aspect of the age of assimilation. Yet the imitators
fail to find their identity in the colonial order, so that in
the second phase a new and estranged political generation
emerges to preach nationalism. It is often at this point, in
the context of less intensive colonial situations (in Egypt,
for instance), that the so-called nation becomes independent. The victorious nationalists, however, have built only
on negative unity; as negators of the colonial order, they
have not had time to redefine their social identity. They
are like Hegel's stubborn slave—with a "mind of their
own" that does not get beyond the attitude of the servant
—not having "endured absolute fear" and allowed their
social substance to be "infected through and through"
with the "negative reality" of utter subjection. Typically
their national image is one of a mythical past, golden but
unreconstructible. Their ties with their own people are
sentimental and fragile; there is no continuous political
structure and no shared mystique of activism that might
procreate symbols of legitimacy.

But when the stakes are high, independence does not
come easily. Instead of yielding, the colonial power may
try to repress the young nationalist movement and, in so
doing, help elicit the third stage of the dialectic. At this
point a new political generation displaces the upper-class
lawyers, professional people, and traditional notables who
had fathered nationalism. The new leaders are more
effective in their protest against the colonial order. Instead of preaching, they foster a widespread sense of
political mission and organize the means to carry it out,
in a modern mass party. Ties with the people go beyond
sentimentality or cynicism, at least initially, because the
culture of the new nation resurrected within the party is
that of the activist who is "sprung from the people."
National identity is founded on the living solidarity of

"all the people" mobilized for combat; history means progress rather than the return to a mythical past.

Resistance to the colonial order is now able to take an authentically dialectical form, the vast power of negation being shaped into an honest affirmation of the colonizer's central values. While national identity is still defined by opposition to colonial domination, the new generation contains within it and surpasses the two previous "moments" of the dialectic: assimilation and rejection of the colonizer's values and way of life. In the rejuvenated opposition, based on a sense of mission, the older assimilation acquires further focus. The notion of individuality implicit in the assimilation of Western ways becomes explicit, because the colonized people now have the opportunity to achieve individuality as political militants taking responsibilities and making choices. The style of protest, too, has been taken from domestic metropolitan politics: typically the new nationalist mass party is modeled on the party of the alienated proletariat, though, as colonial conflict persists, the nationalists are made aware of the political differences dividing the industrial working class from the "proletariat" of the *tiers monde*. Most importantly, through protracted conflict the new nation acquires the symbols of future legitimacy—not only a "charismatic" leader but an equally charismatic party[25]—and a redefinition—by making history—of its identity.

The full play of the dialectic reinforces the modernizing trends implicit in the intensive colonial situation. With the third moment of the dialectic, the nationalists no longer misinterpret all colonial innovations as threats constituting designs for further domination. Rather, while their new sense of mission inspires them to intensify their opposition to colonial rule, their rejection of the situation is a focused and reasoned one. It is the domination itself that is being rejected, not its superficial signs or symptoms as well. Perhaps in order to fully unmask as well as to combat Western domination, one must have assimilated the moral grounds on which it was so ambivalently based. Thus, while it is always true that the colonial power prepared the ground for its own overthrow, it is in the name of the metropolitan social and political values that domination is most decisively and definitively eradicated. Not only are modern values as well as implements accepted: the emancipated nation that has worked through the dialectic is relatively confident of its individuality and can therefore accept further innovations from abroad, without fears of domination or "neo-colonialism."

If the dialectic fully unfolds, the nationalists will have succeeded even before independence in establishing an organized political system—the *pays réel,* represented by a network of auxiliary organizations supplementing the party—as a viable alternative to the colonial *pays légal.* Significantly, too, the resulting integration of the nation may rest upon the active consensus of an elite sufficiently challenged by the traditionalists to have thought out its national objectives.[26] Obviously the process, involving a deep ideological transformation, requires a great deal of time. And for political organizations to develop fully, the "dialectic" should occur in an atmosphere relatively free of violence.

The party experiencing the full play of the dialectic before independence has less need to stress national integration after it attains power, though of course integration is a continuing problem. The party may also put less stress on a self-conscious ideology, if the dialectic actually elicited a broad consensus (at least among the educated elite) on concrete objectives to pursue after independence. Though the colonial dialectic cannot satisfactorily explain all of the structural and ideological variations of mass party regimes, it may account for some. The party emerging from a specially intensive colonial situation will tend, like the patron party emerging from a nonintensive situation, to de-emphasize ideological imagery and structure, though for different reasons. The former enters, as it were, a post-ideological age; it is the accepted symbol of a nation that is already well integrated and hence has less need to justify its rule. Similarly, mass organization is less necessary; tacit consensus may partially replace the rhythmic applause of engineered solidarity. The party does not have to orchestrate the general will every day.

The ideologies of all mass party regimes naturally proclaim the primacy of politics in development. After all, it was primarily through political methods that the parties achieved independence. Moreover, the primacy of politics means that everything is possible that is desired enough. Seemingly impossible tasks, such as the creation of a homogeneous society (nationhood) or economic development, can all be accomplished quickly through mass enthusiasm and diplomacy. Party leaders thus maintain their status based on their experience as mass organizers and negotiators with the colonial power.

Populism and the primacy of politics serve as ideas for maintaining the legitimacy of the party after independence as an instrument for rule. Divested of its class basis, Leninist doctrine provides a convenient formula for party supremacy by reconciling democracy with party dictatorship, while it provides a reassuring explanation of economic backwardness. Thus some mass party regimes have both openly advocated democratic centralism and party dictatorship and decried the dangers of neo-colonialism. Neo-Leninism might be considered the "natural" ideology for mass party regimes.

But this is true only of some of these regimes. Others,

as in Tunisia and Senegal, have stressed alternative perspectives (Bourguibism, *négritude*) that in no way justify one-party rule or dictatorship—which indeed may intellectually embarrass the rulers. Though all the regimes favor some kind of "Socialism," they are agreed neither on the means nor on the source of the difficulties in building it. In Tunisia, neo-colonialism is considered more as a political slogan and a means of excusing the inadequate performances of the slogan-makers than as a serious conceptual category.

Underlying the ideological variations—and the product of differing colonial situations—key structural differences come to light. They concern both the internal organization of the ruling party and the relations between the party and the new state.

The neo-Leninist parties make a cult of organization. The citizen—and often even the child—has no choice in the matter of belonging to the party and its relevant ancillary organization. The rhythm of party activity is permanent and intensive. It requires a substantial bureaucratic apparatus, though in theory the leaders of the party hierarchy are freely elected by the delegates of lower echelons. Actually we do not know enough about the organization, for example, of the Guinean PDG, to describe exactly how decisions are taken or how leaders are elected. Usually "democratic centralism" means that the party bureaucracy, controlled by the general secretary, can successfully engineer the elections of subordinate echelons. It may also often be the case that the secretariat makes key decisions without consulting the rank and file. The myth of democratic participation, however, justifies the rigid discipline expected of party members in executing the decisions. It is in this sense that dictatorship may be "democratic."

"Democracy" is maintained by rigidly subordinating the state to the party, i.e., the Political Bureau or its weightier part. The state is strictly limited, in theory at least, to the implementation of policies decided upon by the party. In Touré's words, the state has "only the tasks of indispensable organization." It is the body but the party is the brain. Ministers must obey the Political Bureau, except on "matters of detail."

Such a theory of the exercise of power, of course, is applicable at best to the small cohesive Rousseauian community where the general will may be expressed clearly and frequently and where problems of political organization are relatively simple. Even if the Political Bureau is taken to express the general will, the ambiguity as to what constitute "details" remains. Faced with conflicts between the party apparatus and the new state administration, Guinea moved after 1960 toward a symbiosis of the two—the state *commandant* of the region, for instance, becoming an *ex officio* member of the party's regional *comité directeur*. In the context of the party's supremacy, of course, the elected parliament had little to do except to provide party decisions with "a legal form that permits practical application."[27] Nor are the party's auxiliary organizations allowed much effective autonomy to mobilize the masses or pursue special interests, much less tacitly to serve as a loyal opposition. For instance, the JRDA (Jeunesse du Rassemblement Démocratique Africain), a youth organization created in 1959 as an arm of the party, eventually had to be placed under the supervision of the Minister of Youth. Similarly, in Mali in 1962, when the party's youth organization was becoming too powerful in its own right, its leader was dismissed from the Political Bureau, its Executive Bureau was abolished, its maximum age limit for members was reduced, and its

local branches were brought under direct local party
control. Whenever an auxiliary becomes too successful as
a mass mobilizer, the party has to curb it—the only
exception to the rule being the Federation of Black
African Students in France (FEANF), whose Paris head-
quarters are out of the reach of any of the mass party
regimes, though they have tried (with little success) to
establish rival student organizations.

Inherent in the neo-Leninist type of regime is the
danger that the party, saddled with administrative responsibilities and becoming increasingly bureaucratic,
may lose all but ritual contact with the people. A further
problem is that by monopolizing all power, the party
tends to exclude trained administrators and technicians
from power and influence. Decisions may be too "political" and not take sufficient account of other realities
equally important, say, to economic development; the
way they are taken may alienate the more technically
minded elite. The price of the primacy of politics is apt to
be a corrosive anti-intellectualism inimical to development.[28]

The alternative to the neo-Leninist model is what might
be called the "permissive" type of mass party regime. It
is hardly described in an ideological formula, and it, too,
has its pitfalls. Party organization is looser: though the
party has a mass membership, it is possible not to be a
member. Of course nonmembers are usually discrimi-
nated against (as in employment and children's education) in the period immediately following independence,
but the state gradually consolidates its authority and
serves as a relatively impartial arbiter. If the party
experienced a lengthy struggle in an intensive colonial
situation, the auxiliary organizations are apt at independence time to be cooperative but relatively autonomous

structures. But they are subsequently brought more fully
under party control—even to the extent as in the neo-
Leninist model of being organically linked to the party.
The party's activity is apt to be less intensive, though
demonstrations and mass information meetings may always be organized for special occasions.

Despite a populist outlook and a belief in the primacy
of politics, the party radically diverges from the Leninist
model after independence by espousing the supremacy of
the new state. The party is tacitly de-emphasized as its
leading cadres leave it for important governmental jobs.
The center of political gravity shifts quite clearly from
party to state, for officials in the latter's apparatus openly
exercise political as well as administrative power. The
party's structure, as in the case of Tunisia in 1958, may
actually be overhauled to ensure its subordination to the
constituted state authorities. The "technicians" are thus
afforded more opportunities for power and rational decision-making.

The price of technocracy, however, is apt to be political
apathy—even for the technocrats who remain dependent
upon the whim of the party (and especially its leader) for
political support. The party apparatus, though possibly
less bureaucratized than that of its neo-Leninist counterpart, does relatively little but "mobilize" the population to
support governmental projects. Hence it acquires a bureaucratic reputation. Fewer people bother to attend the
less frequent meetings, for they feel it represents not them
but the government. To be sure, the party remains a
target for favor-seekers, but it does not attract the political animals of the society and has no way of compelling
them to participate. The "extinct" character of the movement regime becomes visible.

To palliate these deficiencies, the regime may try to

reactivate the party. In 1963, shortly after an abortive plot on his life, Bourguiba hastened to inject his party with a dose of democratic centralism—without, however, explicitly subordinating state to party. In Ghana and even in the Ivory Coast, party supervision committees were installed in government ministries, and Nkrumah recently stressed the need to extend and perfect his party machinery—at the expense, it seemed by early 1964, of his senior civil servants. But ironically the new Algerian regime—which its leaders had insisted would be a paragon of democratic centralist virtue in contrast to bourgeois Tunisia—seems, while trying to rebuild its party, to have opted for state supremacy. Even in Mali, the suppression of the party's national and regional *comités directeurs* in late 1962 (in favor of annual conferences) suggested increasing administrative (governmental) supervision of the party apparatus.

In this fluid state of affairs, it is unrealistic to draw a rigid typology of mass party regimes, subdividing them into the neo-Leninist and "permissive" categories. In the real world mass party regimes resembling one of the types seem also to be acquiring some of the characteristics of the other. Perhaps, too, in the real world of post-independence problems, a mixture of qualities is necessary. For, to summarize, the neo-Leninist model tends to sustain greater party and auxiliary organizational activity, more "mass mobilization" and possibly enthusiasm, but at the cost of a more politicized leadership that by background and temperament is less able to make technically rational decisions.[29] The "permissive" regime, on the other hand, will tend to encourage technical competence and governmental control at the expense of organizational vitality. In both models, however, the very top level of leadership may exercise a restraining and balancing influence on the lower levels; it is here, indeed, where the source of mixture is to be found.

Whatever the proportions of authority accorded to party and to state, all of the mass party regimes—even if we include Algeria, with its classic but unrealized doctrine of collective leadership—share a tendency toward personal power. In some cases, such as the cult of Nkrumah, the tendency is more explicit than in others. Theoretically, in the neo-Leninist model individuals are subordinate to collective institutions. Even Sékou Touré, however, is clearly more than a first among equals.[30] The pattern of acquiring personal power is now familiar. Usually—the exception is Algeria—the independence struggle elicits the emergence of a single leader to hold the party together (or create it) and to serve as a national symbol. With the help of his party after independence, he consolidates his control over the new state; then, with his new power base—and often with the help of the auxiliary organizations—he consolidates his personal ascendancy in the party and then the party's hold over the auxiliaries. The Algerian case offers a variation of the pattern: from his position as head of the new government, attained with the support of the army, Ben Bella tried to re-establish unity among the divided remnants of the FLN—in an unsuccessful effort to keep the army in check.[31]

Obviously the new leaders are all seasoned professional politicians; their "charisma" or prestige is not that of religious prophets or holy men. Unlike the latter, their actions are as explicable in rational political terms as those of any politician. While it *may* be true that some of their more primitive followers view them as holy men, religion is no more a legitimate basis of authority for them inside the party than it was for an Eisenhower. None has a religious message, though each tries by secular means—which may include mass exhortation—to articulate new values for his society. In theocratic societies the leader would inevitably be a far more effective reformer if he were charismatic in the religious sense;[32] but even among the African non-Marxists, religion at most seems a political force to be used, not an autonomous source of inspiration. Nationalism ought not even be psychologically identified with religion, for the leader himself usually outlives his nationalist fervor even while pursuing his secular "calling."

Whatever its causes, personal power seems a characteristic—perhaps a necessary—trait of all mass party regimes. Even when, as in Tunisia, the intensive colonial situation gives rise to a highly cohesive elite, the quasi-omnipotent leader seems indispensable to maintain the cohesion after independence. Often the party may thrive on the cult of the leader just as the latter depends upon the former for political support. The cult provides the party, especially if it is of the non-Leninist variety, with a focus to compensate for the diffuseness of its other roles. Even when the party does not wither away beneath the shadow of the state it created, personal power lends substance to diffuse ideology. In the neo-Leninist regime, however, the supremacy of the leader is assured more by his mastery of the party apparatus and slogans than by an overt personality cult. Organized mass adulation of the leader is more characteristic of regimes fostering state supremacy, because the emphasis upon the leader's role as Head of State provides institutional justification for such adulation.

Prospects

It is in the context of personal power—increasingly evident in the years following independence—that the regime's achievements and prospects must be evaluated. It is by no means evident that "the political parties with institutionalized leadership (mass, as contrasted with patron-type parties) could deal far more smoothly with the problems posed by renewal and succession."[33] The only instance to date of a succession, that of Togo,[34] is hardly reassuring. Even parties with monolithic structures and carefully devised statutes may become paper organizations after a few years of personal power.

Though the tasks we somewhat arbitrarily assigned to mass party regimes are not meant as conditions for these regimes' survival, the ways in which they are met may suggest the direction any given regime is taking. We suggest that there are three possible paths open to these regimes: 1) the regime may stagnate, gradually losing mass loyalties as the party and ancillary organizations wither away in apathy and the government relies on moderate repression to stay in power; 2) the regime may "harden" by transforming the party into a vanguard of highly disciplined militants, devising a revolutionary ideology with chiliastic claims, and perfecting a totalitarian apparatus of systematic repression; or 3) the regime may maintain mass loyalties through perpetual renewal of the party and its related organizations.

In the short run only the first and third seem likely possibilities. It is unlikely that a party mollified by power should suddenly embark upon an adventurous revolutionary path—unless pushed by foreign threats or socially alienated forces within. The angry young intellectuals out of power today might organize a totalitarian revolution tomorrow, but only after a period of stagnation allows for the build-up of a revolutionary situation.

A period of stagnation seems the likeliest prospect. The *embourgeoisement* of the politicians and their progressive divorce from apathetic followers—among the educated elite as well as the masses—is already happening in many of the mass party regimes. Once nominal integration is achieved with the erection of a strong state, the temptation of the leaders is to forego the work of continual recruitment, pursue the tasks of education by ritual, and allow political structures to decay that might have provided genuine representation. The cult of the leader—a form of direct democracy without content—replaces deliberative organs of the party. Procedures within the party—once devised by the leader to stimulate politicization and impress the colonial power and international opinion—are followed only at the leader's convenience. Intent on maintaining his pre-eminent position, the leader plays off factions within the party rather than allowing them to consolidate. The neo-Leninist leader, even if he does not allow a formal personality cult to develop, may even more rigorously suppress factions in the unitarian spirit of Rousseau. Yet without factions—quasi-autonomous power centers—party procedures may at best allow for the voicing of grievances, not for effective deliberation between alternative policies. Without the emergence of coherent factions, too, the succession is apt to be disorderly. Potential rivals learn only how to please the leader, not how to cooperate and compromise with each other. At lower echelons the cadres are apt to become restive or apathetic as they become used to seeing their grievances go unanswered. The auxiliary organizations also lose their appeal as the reality of their subordination to the whim of party managers becomes evident. The ultimate irony of the mass party regime would be for the party in power to become a caucus—the caucus being composed of notables in the leader's entourage rather than traditional patrons. This may be as true of the neo-Leninist model as of other varieties of the mass party regime.

But the countervailing trends are visible that might lead to constitutionalized political renewal in some mass party regimes. By his recent reorganization of the neo-Destour, Bourguiba showed that he saw the dangers of stagnation. The problem in Tunisia was to restore some prestige to a party that had become a mere appendage of the state it had created. In order to effect political renewal, it would seem that the party must be allowed clear-cut channels for influencing state policy; on the other hand, it cannot be allowed actually to exercise the power of the state without becoming simply another bureaucracy. Similarly, the auxiliary organizations must demonstrate clear-cut autonomy and channels of influence. Otherwise, cadres and followers are eventually bound to lose interest in politics or raise the standard of revolt.

Theoretically, a healthy equilibrium that allows a measure of pluralism seems as plausible a prospect as stagnation for mass party regimes. In many of these regimes even today an equilibrium has been reached at the local level whereby party and state have achieved a functional measure of separation. The balance has also allowed the party successfully to pursue the tasks of recruitment, education, integration, and representation. Though the mass party is never sufficiently well-organized and all-encompassing (despite the wishes and exaggerated claims of some politicians) to take the spiritual place of older structures, it can provide a center of social as well as political interest. Party elections as in Guinea at the local level may be genuinely free, in that members commonly are able to choose among candidates at branch elections.

But unfortunately municipal elections are apt as in Tunisia to be rituals in which the elector may vote only for a single party list. Often the party apparatus is able to exercise informal (but legitimate) influence to encourage the election of young new faces in its local branches. Political education consists in teaching villagers to manage their own affairs. They have access to higher party and governmental authorities, who satisfy their demands or explain why they cannot be satisfied. Discussion is encouraged, although, given the villagers' ignorance of alternatives, discussion on national politics is apt to be one-sided.[35]

But in national politics a balance has yet to be struck. Thus far, mass party regimes have failed to provide adequate channels of representation, and therefore recruitment also suffers when once the honeymoon of independence is over.[36] The precondition for any meaningful democracy is the emergence of identifiable (at least to the actors) factions that can provide alternative policies— and leadership in the event of a succession. Thus some accepted formal procedures (though not necessarily the formalized ones of neo-Leninist monoliths) would seem to be essential if decisions are to be reached after a regularized deliberation of alternatives—and not by "mobilization" from above.[37] Publicized meetings at frequent and regular intervals[38] of an extended group of leading party officials and other representative figures would, for instance, be a useful innovation. Parliaments might but usually have not played more than a rubber-stamp role even in states where the party has not pre-empted all policy-making.

The institutionalization of effective deliberation—a first step toward the recognition of a factional politics within the organizations of the mass party regime—may be more likely to materialize, if at all, in regimes where neither party nor state is clearly supreme. If party is supreme, the risks of free deliberation may be too great for those in power; if state is supreme, the potentially deliberative bodies atrophy. In a separation of power situation, on the other hand, the party could conceivably develop deliberative institutions, and ancillary organizations might achieve a measure of autonomy by playing off party and state. Then the regime would be setting up the conditions for the mass party's eventual metamorphosis into a competitive party system.

4

AFRICAN POLITICS
IN
THE UNITED NATIONS

❧

THOMAS HOVET, JR.

The admission of a new member to the United Nations, the arrival of the representative of a new member, and the initial speeches of a new representative invariably stimulate the conversational topics of the "old hands" in the Delegates' Lounge. These initial images both provide an insight into the nature of the new member of "the club" and help in attempting to assess what the new member's impact will be on the organization, processes, and procedures of the United Nations. More important, the role assumed by the new member, both in character and in action, helps to create an image of the country which has been admitted. This paper attempts to analyze various aspects of the participation of Africa in the United Nations as possible avenues of insight into the nature of African politics on the world scene. None of the following observations can provide the whole story. Most of these impressions need further investigation. Such a brief analysis might help, however, in understanding the role of African politics in international politics.

MEMBERSHIP OF THE AFRICAN CAUCUSING GROUP IN THE UNITED NATIONS (Dec. 1964)

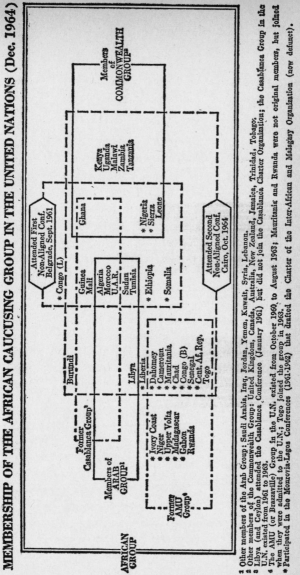

1 Other members of the Arab Group: Saudi Arabia, Iraq, Jordan, Yemen, Kuwait, Syria, Lebanon.
2 Other members of the Commonwealth Group: United Kingdom, Canada, Australia, New Zealand, Jamaica, Trinidad, Tobago.
3 Libya (and Ceylon) attended the Casablanca, Conference (January 1961) but did not join the Casablanca Charter Organization; the Casablanca Group in the U.N. existed from 1961 to 1963.
4 The AMU (or Brazzaville) Group in the U.N. existed from October 1960, to August 1963; Mauritania and Rwanda were not original members, but joined when they were admitted to the U.N.; Togo joined the group in 1963.
* Participated in the Monrovia-Lagos Conferences (1961-1962) that drafted the Charter of the Inter-African and Malagasy Organization (now defunct).

Emergence

It is self-evident that Africa has come onto the United
Nations scene only in the last few years. Excluding South
Africa, there were only three states from the continent
present at the San Francisco Conference in 1945: Ethiopia, Liberia and Egypt (now the United Arab Republic). With the admission of Libya in 1955 and of the
Sudan, Morocco, and Tunisia in 1956, Africa still did not
present an image in the United Nations. The admission of
Ghana in 1957 and of Guinea in 1958 and the conference
of African states in Accra in 1958 for the first time made
an African image apparent. The sudden acceleration of
the independence movement in Africa since the summer
of 1960 has made the UN aware of Africa, especially of
Africa south of the Sahara. Sixteen new African members
were admitted in 1960, three more in 1961, four more in
1962, two more in 1963, and two more in 1964, with even
more African members approaching the threshold of
independence and admission.* The thirty-five African
states form the largest representation from one continent
within the one hundred and fifteen members of the
organization.

The significance of this sudden and large increase in
African membership may lie not so much in the size of
African representation as in the timing of its emergence
in the organization. The fact that Africa came into the
United Nations when it did not only has an impact on the
politics of Africa in the world organization, but also
shapes the impression that the African states make upon
the older members of the United Nations. By 1960, of

* After this was written, Zambia was admitted in September
1965, bringing the number of African states to thirty-six.

course, the UN had experienced and survived, although scarred and altered, many crises and problems. Many of its basic procedures and organizations were already established. "Gentlemens' agreements" had formulated the allocation of elective seats in the Security Council, the Economic and Social Council, the Trusteeship Council, the International Court of Justice, and many other committees and councils. In many instances the formula for election had been revised with difficulty with the earlier admission of a number of Asian members. The relationship between the Security Council, the General Assembly and the Secretary General had undergone a transformation. The deadlock in the Cold War created an East–West axis of conflict in the United Nations that up to 1950, at least, was reflected at every level of the organization and almost left it dormant. The development of Asian nationalism and independence, culminating in the Bandung Conference in 1955, left a strong impact on the United Nations. The major powers at San Francisco in 1945 (the permanent members of the Security Council—China, France, the United Kingdom, the Soviet Union, and the United States) were in reality reduced to two major powers, the United States and the Soviet Union. The organization not only survived the crises of Korea in 1950 and Suez in 1956, but the deadlock over the Secretary Generalship between 1950 and 1953.

The block admission to the organization in 1955 of many states changed the United Nations from a limited organization of sixty members to one approximating universalism. The interests of the newly independent states served to focus the interest of the world body on the problems of the developing countries. The stakes on every issue began to reflect not only an East–West axis of conflict but a North–South axis (i.e., developed versus underdeveloped countries) as well. Moral issues of the rights of man supplanted legal arguments about the exclusion of domestic questions from international concern.

By 1960, when African countries moved into the United Nations in force, the character of the organization had evolved into a center that was ideal for the interests of these newly independent areas. East and West had to accept the importance of the problems of these new nations, and if they could not support their interests they were at least forced to justify their differences. While the atmosphere was favorable to sympathetic discussion of the interests of Africa when it moved into the UN, the older members had already evolved practices of procedures and organization which have presented problems for the new African members. All of these developments before 1960 have had an impact on African politics in the United Nations, an impact that might have been different had Africa not arrived on the scene when it did.

Organization

Compared with other groups of states the African members of the United Nations are more organized in their efforts than any group except the members of the Soviet Bloc. At least they are more *formally* organized to coordinate their policies and actions. (See the table, p. 117.) Behind the scenes of the formal structure of the United Nations there has evolved over the years the formal–informal organization of caucusing groups and blocs. The African caucusing group was first organized in May 1958 following the Accra Conference. It was organized by a formal agreement among the African ambassadors to the United Nations, the only caucusing group having a formal agreement as its basis, although at the time it was organized there were nine other caucusing groups in existence.

Prior to the Accra Conference all the African states had participated in the Afro-Asian caucusing group. Libya, Morocco, Tunisia, and the U.A.R. were also members of the Arab Group, and Ghana had participated in the Commonwealth caucus. Whether the Accra Conference would have organized a structure of caucusing if this informal process had not already been highly developed cannot be ascertained. On the other hand, the African states had much to gain by formally organizing their efforts behind the scenes. By the time Africa had an image in the United Nations with definite interests, the General Assembly had assumed a role that encouraged states to work for prior agreements to build majorities. And in seeking representation on United Nations elective bodies it was very desirable to have a unified position on candidates so that a bloc of votes could be successfully bargained in an election.

With the sudden increase in the African members of the United Nations in 1960, the African caucusing group suddenly jumped from a small caucus of nine members to one of twenty-six at the beginning of the Fifteenth Session of the General Assembly. At the same time the group became to a degree divided, because of the formation within it of two sub-groups—the Brazzaville group and the Casablanca group—that reflected inter-African conferences taking place outside the United Nations.

The Brazzaville or African and Malagasy Union (AMU) caucusing group was created on an *ad hoc* basis in October 1960, became a regular caucusing group in December 1960, and in the spring of 1962 was transformed into a caucusing bloc—that is, a majority of the AMU members could commit all the members of the group to vote a particular way on issues in the General

Assembly. In practice the AMU group did on occasion allow individual members to vote differently from the bloc position. This happened on such questions as problems involving Israel and Chinese refugees. In each instance the bloc majority determined whether to declare the issue one in which there would be a "free" vote. Senegal appears to have requested more "free" votes than any other member of the AMU group.

The creation of the Brazzaville or AMU group was a contributing factor in the creation of the Casablanca caucusing group, which became operative within the African caucusing group in March 1961. The states that met at Monrovia in 1961 and Lagos in 1962 did not, however, form a separate caucusing group within the African group. With the unification of the international organization developments in Africa in the formation of the Organization of African Unity in Addis Ababa in May 1963, the stage was set for the dissolution of the Brazzaville and Casablanca caucuses, which were formally dissolved during the summer of 1963. At present there is only one African caucusing group, which includes all thirty-five African states and which to all intents and purposes is the continuation of the African caucusing group that has been operative since it was first created in May 1958. At the same time some members of the African caucus are still members of the Commonwealth and Arab caucuses, and all members of the African caucusing group are members of the Afro-Asian caucusing group. In addition all of the African states, except Somalia, participated in the UN Conference on Trade and Development (Geneva, March–June 1964) and joined in forming a developing states caucus, known as the "Geneva 75" group; they continue as members of that group at the UN in New York.

The African caucusing group and its so-called informal

Permanent Machinery, as well as the Brazzaville and Casablanca groups when they existed, play a role in facilitating cooperation and coordination in the United Nations, and outside it as well, in regard to planning and implementing the activities of the various inter-African conferences. Prior to the Addis Ababa Conference in 1963, all members of the African caucus worked in the planning stages of such conferences as the Monrovia and Lagos Conferences of 1961–62, including the representatives of states that did not attend these conferences. This dual role of the African caucus, which is more apparent than in any other caucusing group in the United Nations, is a reflection of the fact that the United Nations serves as the center of African diplomatic activity. It serves as a center for discussion of many issues (four to five hundred a year) that are never placed on the formal agendas of the various organs of the United Nations. To newly independent states, such as those African states which have severe budgetary limitations, it is only natural that their representatives to the UN should perform a dual role, serving not only as representatives to the United Nations bodies but as diplomatic contacts to other governments, particularly those to which they cannot afford to maintain embassies and legations. Without this use of the United Nations as a center for worldwide diplomatic contacts, many of the African states would go bankrupt trying to establish a network of embassies and legations, or they would be forced into virtual isolation from dealings with most other countries. This is even true in establishing contacts between the various countries in Africa. Ghana appears to be the only African state making a concerted effort to establish formal diplomatic posts in all other African countries. One member of the Mission of Ghana to the United Nations has commented that this was a policy of "financial silliness."

If any generalization can be made from the many inter-African conferences held since 1958, it is that they have had an almost identical concern with international problems. While the divisions created by the Casablanca and Brazzaville series of conferences differed more in degree of action, even they expressed similar concerns. The Addis Ababa Conference re-emphasized, however, the need for a coordinated approach of the African states in the United Nations. In a very real sense the mood of Africa transmitted to the African caucus by the 1963 Addis Ababa Conference was a mandate for procedures to make the African voice in the United Nations a voice of unity. As Mr. Lansana of Guinea explained to the Eighteenth Session of the General Assembly:

It is our conviction that the African delegations, contrary to their recent past, will deem it their duty to speak not only the same words, but to give to their statements the same content which will reflect, despite the diversity of forms of expression and psychological variants which distinguish us, an identical awareness and a common will to affirm forcefully to the world the personality and the *raison d'être* of Africa within the concert of the United Nations. The African delegations will no longer be defined in their relations with each other by standards of negation, because they are determined no longer to play the game of dividers of Africa and far less to be subject of covetous and Machiavellian plans of those who would substitute themselves to direct colonialism, which has been fought against by our peoples, in concealed forms which entail no less indignity and subjugation for our peoples.

It is our comfort that all African delegations will henceforth speak but the language of Africa, that is to say, the language of historical truth aroused by an acute sense of responsibility and a powerful force of general renewal of Africa in its own context.

. . . Among the agenda items that concern the evolution

of our continent, the statements of several African delegations
will complete each other; the entire African group will present itself in a homogeneous and intangible form.[1]

To an observer of the Eighteenth Session of the Assembly
it appears that the coordination of the policies and
actions of the African group is more evident than ever in
the past.

From its beginning the African group has limited its
concerns and actions to African questions, and has made
every effort not to become a lobby within the larger Afro-
Asian group, except on African questions. This policy
was reaffirmed at the Addis Ababa Conference. Operative
paragraph four of the resolution on Africa and the United
Nations adopted at Addis Ababa reaffirms this relationship with the Afro-Asian Group:

[The Conference . . .] *further invites* African Governments to instruct their representatives in the United Nations,
without prejudice to their membership in and collaboration
with the African-Asian Group, to constitute a more effective
African Group with a permanent secretariat to bring about
closer cooperation and better coordination in matters of common interest.

Since the Addis Ababa Conference, and particularly since
the dissolution of the Brazzaville and Casablanca groups,
the African Group has been proceeding with steps to
transform the "informal permanent machinery" of the
African group into more "permanent machinery." A
crucial question in the process of strengthening the media
of cooperation and coordination of the group has been
whether it should remain a caucusing group, in which
there is discussion to reach a nonbinding consensus, or
whether it should become a caucusing bloc in which a
majority of the group could commit the votes of the entire
membership, as was done by the Brazzaville Group. At

present this problem does not appear to have been resolved. In a sense it may be moot if the consensus on
African issues is easily arrived at, and this may depend
upon the degree to which the desire for unity on international questions expressed at Addis Ababa persists.

Representation

While it may be difficult if not impossible to attempt
generalizations about the image Africa presents at the
United Nations through its representatives, there are
points warranting consideration.

In the most general sense the African delegates to the
UN have brought candor and frankness into the discussion of international issues. They appear to have no
hesitation in saying what they mean. They leave their
innuendoes at home and meet most questions openly. A
few excerpts from the discussions in the Eighteenth Session of the Assembly might illustrate this point. Discuss-
ing suggestions to the developed countries about ways to
aid the developing countries, Mr. Kambona of Tanganyika said:

First, the practice of the mercantile system must come to
an end.

Second, we need capital for development. But very often
the donors of capital say: "I am making you the loan. You
must not only repay the loan, plus interest on it, you must also
use the loan to buy my goods. . . ." Sometimes the donors
go so far as to say: "I want your vote in the United Nations."
This is neo-colonialism.[2]

Few diplomats have spoken as frankly about the pressures
placed on the way they cast their votes. States may be
disappointed with the policies of other countries, but

seldom have the diplomats stated their disappointments as have the Africans. Following a debate in the Special Political Committee on the apartheid policies of South Africa, the delegate of Guinea characterized the votes of other countries very frankly:

. . . The attitude of the white partners of the Commonwealth, the United Kingdom, Australia, Canada and New Zealand, was a matter of deep disappointment to us. They seem to have abandoned their coloured partners in the Commonwealth, who will certainly know how to draw the necessary conclusions from this attitude. So far as Panama is concerned, we hope that in the General Assembly it will add its positive vote to those of the rest of the Latin Americans. Finally, the abstention of the United States of America surprised and pained us by depriving us of their great influence in the cause of racial equality in South Africa. We wish the United States would reconsider its position of yesterday, if only not to inflict such a denial on numerous delegations, among them that of the Republic of Guinea who, from this rostrum and elsewhere, congratulated the Kennedy Administration for its courageous fight against racial discrimination in this country.[3]

The bluntest statements are of course reserved for comments on South Africa and Portugal. Following a speech by the South African representative, Mr. Wachuku, the Foreign Minister of Nigeria, has stated:

I want to say that my delegation was much surprised to hear from the representative of the minority Government of South Africa that they have no official information of what is going on in their own country. Anybody who has read *The Times* of London, the *Daily Telegraph* of London, the *New York Times*, and other papers must have familiarized himself with these prosecutions that have been staged in South Africa, and for a representative of a state to tell us here that . . .

he knows nothing officially about it, is to tell us that the speaker is not the official representative of his own State.[4]

Or, speaking on Portugal, the representative from Senegal (Mr. Thiam) has said:

Since we began to speak of the Portuguese colonies in this Assembly, there is hardly anything we have not heard. In rereading the statements made by the various spokesmen of the Portuguese Government, one can see with what tremendous patience we have dealt with this question in this high international forum. During the debate in the plenary meetings of the General Assembly in December 1960, Mr. Vasco de Garin, the representative of Portugal, told us that his country was four centuries ahead of all others in the field of decolonization. The hypocrisy of the policy of assimilation is thus changed all at once into blatant provocation. "Four centuries ahead in the field of colonization," indeed. It is we who are stupid and who do not understand anything; it is we who are four centuries behind Portugal. We may be compelled soon to admit that the newly independent States and their former metropolitan Powers are retrogressive, and that the whole work of decolonization undertaken by France, Great Britain and the Netherlands will have to start all over again. . . .[5]

Out of context these examples of candor may not seem blunt and frank, but within the traditional form of diplomatic debate in the UN they are refreshing. They do not have the bitter sharpness of the propaganda attacks of the Soviet Bloc countries at the height of the Cold War, but they have the intellectual sharpness that one finds in sophisticated debates in established parliaments.

The typical meeting of the African Group is filled with what might appear to the outsider as some sort of organized chaos, replete with brutally frank statements, in which all that is felt is said. Yet this vocal catharsis, rather than ending in lasting bitterness, results in consensus and harmony. Such a process of negotiation is a welcome addition to United Nations diplomacy.

The candor of the African representatives is apparent in many other ways. In informal discussions behind the scenes it is even more impressive. They seem to have little sense of state security, and are perfectly willing to divulge the most intimate details of negotiations and the most particular aspects of the decision-making process within their governments. There is more discretion on the ambassadorial level, but even here candor and frankness seem to be more apparent than in the case of any other delegation to the United Nations. What will be the ultimate effect of this candor on the organization is not easy to determine.

Another characteristic of the African representative is a result of his newness in the UN. For the most part African representatives lack a background of knowledge of the development and evolution of the processes, procedures, and problems before the United Nations. Older delegates, especially those who attended the 1945 San Francisco Charter Conference, may be more tolerant of the limitations of the Charter and more understanding of the difficulties in implementing its goals. An African delegate may listen to the discussion of the relevance of a particular Article of the Charter and may pose questions evidencing a complete lack of understanding of that document. South Africa, for example, may argue, supported by the United Kingdom, that the consideration of an issue is in violation of the "domestic jurisdiction clause" of Article 2, paragraph 7, of the Charter. The African delegate may counter this argument in the formal debate, but privately ask over lunch, "Just what is this Article 2 (7) all about?" Session after session of the UN may have considered the question of Korean unification, or the problem of Palestine refugees, but the new African

delegate may stun his listener in his cocktail conversation
with a question of "What's this thirty-eighth parallel?" or
"Where did all the refugees come from?" This naïveté
may be only transitional, but it is indicative of the
problem that plagues the newly arrived African delegate.
He has to brief himself not only on the currently relevant
aspects of an issue but also on the background of the
problem, and more importantly on the background and
development of the procedures and processes of the
Charter and the United Nations. In some respects it is
useful to subject these processes and procedures to basic
questions, but it may lead to confusion and to a complica-
tion of the procedures. It may even raise questions about
the competence of the delegate.

A more serious problem for the procedures of the
United Nations arises from the difficulties in the negotiating process caused by the large number of African delegations that have French as their only working language.
Prior to the admission of these French-speaking African
delegates, the chief working language of the UN had
gradually become English. Even the meetings of the
African and Afro-Asian caucuses have become complicated by the presence of so many French-speaking delegates. Often draft proposals in English may be "amended"
when translated into French, but the French amendments make no sense when translated back into English.
Debates and confusion on semantics are thus added to the
discussions on the substance of issues. The tendency
toward bilingualism in French and English seems slow in
developing among the African states. This language problem is more crucial in the process of informal negotiation
than in the formal sessions where it is overcome by the
interpretation system. In a sense it serves to isolate the
French-speaking African delegates, and their isolation
creates some reservations about their motivations. It also

adds to the suspicion that they are more closely allied to France than may be the case.

African representation in the United Nations is also typified by either the "overworked delegate" or the "indifferent delegate." Many of the delegations are small either for financial reasons or the hesitation to assign skilled individuals to posts of continual duty outside their countries. If the delegate is conscientious he is occupied in a backbreaking task of attending, almost simultaneously, several meetings at the same time that he is engaged in background research on an issue and drafting statements on a current problem. Often the delegate to the General Assembly may continue to serve in another governmental post and may be faced not only with following issues at the United Nations but at the same time with conducting, via mail and telegram, his regular government assignment. If he is not conscientious, other delegations may tend to look upon him with disdain for his lack of background knowledge and preparation, and for the flippant manner in which he assumes his role in the UN. Both of these instances are extremes. More often the overall impression is amazement at the high degree of competence and skill of the African delegates, particularly in view of their youth and inexperience. It is almost as if they had a sixth sense of what is required in the United Nations, and while they may lack background knowledge they perform their tasks with an innate sense of the role of a diplomat in this continuous multilateral conference with more efficiency than many representatives with more experience in the United Nations.

There is little doubt that some of the African representatives see the assignment to the United Nations as an opportunity for personal prestige. This may be a reflection of the policies of their country. The forum of the world is available and it is an easy step for a state or a delegate to use it to achieve a place in the world spotlight. The vocal image created before this spotlight may give an aura of power that far exceeds the actual power position of the country. Ghana has assumed such a role in the UN, a role that probably in the public image exceeds its actual importance in international politics. The ambassador of at least one African state has carefully used his position to create an impression of importance that far exceeds his abilities. He even plays musical chairs by continually shifting the responsibilities of his subordinates in the delegation so that none of them will attain a competence that may challenge his share of the spotlight. On the other hand, some African delegations, such as Tunisia's, have gained deserved international prestige by the quiet but vital role of conciliator they have assumed behind the scenes in the process of facilitating all kinds of negotiations. This sort of respect, which is almost universally felt for the quiet skill of the Tunisian delegation, may do more to enhance the prestige of their country and Africa than all the skills of showmanship.

Lastly, it should be noted that the inclusion of many women on the African delegations has more than doubled the number of women participating in the diplomatic processes of the United Nations. By comparison the African delegations provide more equal opportunities for women than most other delegations. The first woman to be elected to the chairmanship of a politically oriented main committee was Miss Angie Brooks of Liberia, who several years ago was elected to preside over the workings of the Fourth Committee. Previously women had only rarely been elected to committee posts and generally only on the Social Committee. Mrs. Huguette Achard of Dahomey was elected to the important post of rapporteur of the Special Political Committee in the Eighteenth Session of the Assembly and did an excellent job.

Concerns

To any observer it is apparent that the major concern of
the African members of the UN is the elimination of
colonialism and discrimination in Africa. Secondarily
they are concerned with the elimination of colonialism
everywhere, the promotion of human rights, and steps to
foster and encourage the economic and social development of the underdeveloped areas of the world. To a
degree, the concentration on African-rooted problems is
viewed by some delegates as a parochial outlook. The
concentration of interest and pressure on Portugal and
South Africa has often resulted in an exclusion of an
African interest in the many other problems plaguing the
United Nations. The African concern is understandable
and justified, but while these concerns are paramount, it
is also evident that there is some direct relationship
between the number of years an African state has been
in the United Nations and its tendency to broaden its
interests to include other items on the agenda. African
states with longer service in the United Nations begin to
see the relationship between a solution of the problems of
armaments and the increased availability of funds for
development purposes. If one compares the speeches of
the African states in the General Debate in the General
Assembly in 1960 and 1963, it is very evident that their
interests have gradually, but surely, broadened to include
issues that are not directly related to Africa. This development appears to have deeper motivations than the
simple necessity of supporting the interests of other
groups in order to build voting majorities on issues of
prime concern to Africa. Rather, Africa seems to be more
aware of the interrelationship of international issues.

Strategy and Tactics

A fundamental point of departure in the achievement of African policy interests in the United Nations is the effort of the African states to obtain seats in the elective bodies. The General Assembly and its main committees are the only bodies in which all members have representation. The six nonpermanent members of the Security Council, all eighteen members of the Economic and Social Council, some nonadministrative members of the Trusteeship Council, and the fifteen judges of the International Court of Justice are elected by the General Assembly. In addition, the General Assembly elects its General (or Steering) Committee and other procedural Committees, and the Economic and Social Council elects the membership of its many committees and commissions. There is considerable competition among the various caucusing groups in elections to these bodies, as each desires to have adequate representation on these important organs.

During the first part of the First Session of the General Assembly a number of so-called "Gentlemens' agreements of 1946" were reached informally by the delegations. They essentially provide formulas for the distribution of seats on most of these less-than-full-membership bodies. In the case of the six elective seats on the Security Council, the "gentlemen's agreement" provided that one seat would go to Western Europe, two to Latin America, one to the Commonwealth, one to Eastern Europe, and one to the Middle Eastern (or Arab) states. Comparable formulas were agreed upon for the other major organs. As the organization gradually expanded in the 1950's from fifty to eighty-two members (prior to the large increase in African members) the newly admitted Asian states pressed for a reallocation of this distribution of elective seats among the various political areas. The difficulty of agreeing upon a new formula for each body resulted in occasional bitter contesting for seats, but for the most part it was impossible to get any group that had representation to agree to an alteration in the particular formula. In the case of the committees and commissions of the Economic and Social Council and the General Committee of the General Assembly it was possible to enlarge the size of the membership of these bodies by amendments to the rules of procedure and thus to enlarge the formulas without eliminating the representation of any group with previous representation. But it was impossible to enlarge the Security Council, the Economic and Social Council, the Trusteeship Council, and the International Court of Justice to accommodate an expanded formula unless there was a formal amendment to the Charter. Any amendment to the Charter requires the concurrence of the five permanent members of the Security Council. While these possible amendments to the Charter have been continually on the agenda of the General Assembly since 1956, the Soviet Union has consistently opposed (and therefore blocked) any possible amendment unless and until the question of Chinese representation in the various organs of the United Nations is resolved.

The net result of all this is that, having arrived on the scene long after the initial election formulas were negotiated, Africa has not been guaranteed representation on these organs. In general, without a hard, bitter, and impossible fight, the only African states that will be elected will be those that fit within the 1946 agreements. In the Security Council, for example, Ghana may be elected to the Commonwealth seat, or Morocco to the Middle Eastern (or Arab) seat. On occasion an election battle may result in a deadlock with a member of another group, which will be resolved with the two contesting states each serving one year of the two-year term as a compromise. Such election fights, which are tied up in national prestige, create bitterness that often transfers itself into substantive issues.

It is very important that the African states in the UN obtain representation on these organs. The African Group, with thirty-five members, can logically argue that it is the largest geographical group in the United Nations and has a right to adequate representation.[6]

Increasingly the inter-African conferences have stressed in their resolutions the need for the African states to have adequate representation in the less-than-full-membership bodies. The 1963 Addis Ababa Conference in particular stressed these demands. The United States had argued for amendments to the Charter, but the Soviet Union has argued for an alteration of the formulas, suggesting that the representation of Latin America be decreased. The African states, however, are hesitant to work against the Latin Americans because they are potential allies on substantive issues of common interest to underdeveloped countries. The frustration of Africa is typified in the plea of Mr. Wachuku of Nigeria to the Eighteenth Session of the General Assembly in 1963:

We have tried to ask for an amendment of the Charter—just another amendment—to increase the number of members in the Security Council—to increase the number, that is all; we do not want a total overhaul of the Charter. Everybody agrees that that would be a good thing except certain Powers that say it would be so only if China comes in. We say this is irrelevant to the issue.

Then, in the absence of an amendment to enlarge, to enable us to have our representation—reallocate the existing seats. With respect to the 1946 Gentlemen's Agreement, again the answer is "no." May I ask this Assembly, Mr. President, through you, does this Organization want thirty-two African States to be just vocal members, with no right to be able to express their views on any particular matter in important organs of the United Nations? Are we only going to continue to be veranda boys? This matter must be settled at this session one way or another.

Thirty-two independent African States want their own representation in these various organs. We fought last year on principle. At one time we were told that Africa and the Middle East had a seat. We tested that. And this Assembly decided that the seat was a Middle Eastern seat. We have decided not to look to any other seat as belonging to Africa. Africa has none.

Today the position is that Europe has three permanent seats and two non-permanent seats. Asia has one permanent seat. The Americas have one permanent seat and two non-permanent seats. The Middle East has one non-permanent seat. The Commonwealth has one non-permanent seat. Africa, with thirty-two States: nil. . . .

I am appealing to the Europeans, both East and West. This division of Eastern Europe and Western Europe is unreal. There is only one Europe—we all learn geography— there is only one Europe. I am appealing to you—Europe— to give us two non-permanent seats. One permanent seat is more powerful than twenty non-permanent seats because it has the right of veto.

Therefore, I am saying here—I want it on the record— my delegation feels that Europe is more adequately represented in the Security Council. And if they are not prepared to agree to amend the Charter, just to enlarge it to give us our seat, then be gracious enough to surrender those two non-permanent seats to Africa so that we may have a voice in this organ of the United Nations.

We do not want any conflict with Latin America. Latin America, like Africa, is one of the underdeveloped areas, or developing countries as they call us; we have a common disability. Why should we go and rob them of their seats? We do not want to take anything from Latin America. They are twenty States. They have occupied the seats. Therefore, no one should play us against anyone.

My delegation strongly feels that the Gentlemen's Agreement, if we are not going to amend the Charter for the purpose of enlarging it, should be changed at this session. If it is not a gentlemen's agreement, let it be a lady's [sic] agreement. We have ladies in various delegations at this time. If the gentlemen will not agree, I am sure the ladies will agree that Africa is entitled to these seats.[7]

In some respects, the African states were successful in the Eighteenth Session of the General Assembly in their drive for adequate representation. After at least six weeks of intensive negotiation they succeeded in obtaining the passage of a resolution enlarging the General Committee from twenty-one to twenty-five. In addition, over the objections of France and the Soviet Union, they succeeded in getting the Assembly to adopt proposed amendments to the Charter by which the Security Council would be increased from eleven to fifteen members, and the Economic and Social Council from eighteen to twenty-seven. Obviously these amendments would not take effect unless and until they were formally ratified by two thirds of the members of the UN, including the five permanent members of the Security Council. On the final vote on this resolution France and the Soviet Union voted against the question and the other permanent members—China, the United Kingdom, and the United States—abstained. So in spite of the adoption of the proposals by the Assembly the likelihood of their being ratified was remote, unless France and the Soviet Union changed their views and the other permanent members gave their active support. In the negotiations leading up to the resolution for amendment the African states did succeed in weakening the opposition of the Soviet Bloc. Several African diplomats visited

Peking and reported to the Assembly that the People's Republic of China did not want the question of Chinese representation to hinder efforts to enlarge these two councils. Assisted by this development and other statements from Peking on the question, the Eighteenth Session saw one of the Soviet Bloc members, Albania, argue against the position of the Soviet Union, and in the final plenary discussion it seemed as if the Soviet position was changing. By early 1964 it was rumored around the UN that the Soviet Union might ratify the proposed amendments. It then became apparent that the major obstacle was France, as well as the failure of the United Kingdom and the United States to define their policy on the question. As late as April 1964, a spokesman of the United States mission stated that the U.S. still had not made a policy decision on the problem. However, the African pressure continued and after the Soviet Union ratified the amendments the other major powers did also, and by August 31, 1965, the amendments had been ratified and the Security Council was increased to fifteen and the Economic and Social Council to twenty-seven. At the same time, the African Group was successful in its efforts to get enlargement (and representation) on the General Committee and other committees of the Assembly and the Economic and Social Council. The size of these bodies could be changed by modifications in the rules of procedure rather than by amendments to the Charter. Pending these amendments, the African Group was actually successful in getting the Ivory Coast elected to the seat that has traditionally been held by members of the Commonwealth.

The importance of obtaining adequate representation in these main organs lies in the fact that the ability of Africa to achieve proper consideration of its policy interests may be dependent upon this step of procedure. Africa has

often been frustrated in its ability to try to place items on
the agenda of the Security Council, and adequate African
representation there might alter the situation. The problem has a deeper meaning, however, because it affects
African attitudes toward the older members of the United
Nations. To the African Group this fight for adequate
representation on all of the organs of the UN has a
similarity to the nationalist fight for recognition as an
independent and sovereign state. Continual frustration
could alter the tactics and strategy, if not the policies, of
the African Group on a wide variety of substantive issues.
An indication of the type of future action that the African
Group would support can be seen in the Committee on the
Implementation of the Declaration on the Elimination of
Colonialism—the so-called Committee of Twenty-Four.
Created by the General Assembly in 1961 (as a Committee of Seventeen, enlarged to twenty-four in 1962), this
Committee has to all intents and purposes become a
seventh main organ of the United Nations. Even the
Trusteeship Council has been required to report to this
Committee. The African and Asian states constitute sixteen of its twenty-four members, a more adequate reflection of equitable representation. Assuming the role of a
major organ of the United Nations, the Committee has
come in for considerable criticism from the older (and
European) members of the UN, who protest that it has
assumed too much power. But this tendency to support
authority for committees not expressly envisioned in the
Charter may continue unless the Africans are given an
opportunity to participate in the main Charter organs of
the United Nations.

In a more general sense the tactics of Africa in the
United Nations are conditioned by the types of issues
with which it has a primary concern. Questions of the
achievement of self-determination and the promotion of

fundamental human rights, and even of assistance to the economic and social development of underdeveloped countries, can be considered moral issues, and tactically the African states assume the offensive on these issues in relation to the degree to which they can present them as moral issues. And where there is a moral issue, the African states can place objecting states in a very defensive position, almost a position of embarrassment. Certainly, the African states are constantly trying to force this role on objecting states. The United States and the United Kingdom are continually forced to explain that their sympathy lies with the policies of the African states, and then mumble some technical reasons why they are unable to support the African policies. And eventually the United States and the United Kingdom find this indefensible and gradually come to support the African position. The African tactics in this sense have been fairly successful. By December 4, 1963, for example, the Security Council unanimously passed a resolution condemning South Africa and asking all governments to end the sale and shipment of equipment and materials for making and maintaining arms and ammunition in South Africa.

In dealing with African issues before the United Nations, the African states stress all the issues at the same time. The pressure is continually on South Africa, Portugal, Britain, and Southern Rhodesia. Yet beneath the surface there appears to be a well-conceived timetable of priorities. The major efforts are concentrated first on Portugal and the situations in Angola and Portuguese Guinea (less on that in Mozambique). Pressure on Portugal takes the form of requests for definitive actions by the United Nations, alternated with efforts to give Portugal an opportunity to adjust its policies. In public there are demands for immediate action by Portugal; behind-the-

scenes overtures are extended to seek a change in Portuguese policies with a face-saving device. Second on the
priority list appears to be the question of South West
Africa, though for the moment pressure is a bit relaxed
pending the decision of the International Court on the
cases on South West Africa. Last on the timetable of
priorities appears to be a direct push on the situation in
South Africa. Certainly a changed situation in the Portuguese colonies, if not in South West Africa, would increase in itself the pressures on South Africa.

While this timetable is long-range, it does not mean that
every opportunity for continual pressure for the elimination of colonialism in Africa will not continue to be
seized. Another element affecting this sequence of goals is
the apparent recognition by the African Group that it is
not sufficient for them to push for the adoption of resolutions which might not be implemented because they do
not have the support of the states in the UN that would be
necessary to implement the resolutions. Vocally, at every
opportunity, the African states request the most extreme
form of sanctions to compel South Africa and Portugal to
abide by the many, many resolutions passed by the
General Assembly on their policies. But behind the scenes
the African states seem willing to modify their demands
in an effort to carry along the United States and the
United Kingdom. There is a step-by-step concept in this
process of adjustment, each resolution slowly but surely
going a step further. In the Seventeenth Session of the
Assembly, for example, the draft resolution requested
states to take certain actions with regard to South Africa,
such as breaking diplomatic relations and certain other
measures. However, after the request to states in the
resolution, the phrase "in conformity with the Charter"
was inserted, so that states that might want to support the

spirit of the resolution could do so even though they felt it was not in conformity with the Charter for the General Assembly, rather than the Security Council, to recommend such actions. Thus states that would be needed for any real attempt to impose sanctions could at least tag along by abstaining. The next step was taking the questions to the Security Council, where another resolution accepted in modified form requested the stoppage of arms shipments to South Africa; the tactics paid off when the United States somewhat reluctantly supported the proposal. Step by step the resolutions are drawing nearer to outright sanctions, each step gradually shifting the positions of states like the United States and the United Kingdom, which would have to support willingly any eventual sanctions against South Africa if they were to be enforceable. Behind the vocal demands of the African states towards Portugal and South Africa are long-range insights into how to achieve their goals.

At times the vocal tactics may seem disrupting, as in the recent walk-outs and demands for the expulsion of South Africa and Portugal from the United Nations. Expulsion is vocally threatened, but the strategy appears to force the ouster of South Africa and Portugal from technical and scientific bodies and conferences from which they derive some benefits, while at the same time keeping them on a hot seat within the United Nations. Thus moves were made in the summer of 1963 in the International Labor Organization, the United Nations Conference on Map Problems in Africa, the UNESCO-sponsored Twenty-sixth International Conference on Education, the United Nations Economic Commission for Africa, the United Nations Conference on Tourism, and the International Union for the Conservation of Natural and General Resources which resulted in either the ouster or withdrawal

of South Africa and Portugal from these meetings. The
policy in the United Nations itself has been explained as
follows:

Their expulsion would serve no useful purpose at all.
It would be a waste of time. It is better to bring them here
and keep on whipping them until they have learned their
lesson. To throw them outside and leave them in the cold
would just relieve them of this real burden. If members of an
organization do not want to observe the rules of the organization, the only way you can teach them a lesson is to bring
them up every time and expose them to a certain amount of
humiliation and indignity, and one day they will learn some
sense.[8]

In addition to putting consistent pressure on South
Africa and Portugal, the African Group members have
continually supported nationalist groups in the remaining
colonial areas in Africa, complementing the machinery
established at the 1963 Addis Ababa Conference to support these nationalist movements. Representatives of the
nationalist movements are brought to the United Nations
as members of certain African delegations, where generally they are listed as advisers. By this process these
nationalist groups are provided with a basis of access to
the other United Nations members. It is possible on
almost any day to establish contact in the Delegates'
Lounge with nationalist movement representatives from
virtually all the remaining colonial areas in Africa. They
can provide the vocal ammunition for UN debates on
conditions in these areas.

Traditionally, as we have seen, the African states in the
United Nations have confined their major negotiating
efforts to African issues, but by 1963 it had become
apparent that they were aware that they must concern
themselves with other issues in order to build support for

their viewpoints on African issues. They have at the same
time made more thorough efforts to see that most other
delegations are aware of the details of an African issue,
rather than concentrate on explaining their positions in
the public discussions. They have begun to move out of a
preoccupation with African questions to a tactical understanding that one gets support when one gives support,
and that this applies particularly to states whose support
is necessary for the implementation of any resolution.

Cohesion

Only brief consideration will be given to the degree of
cohesion of the African states in the United Nations
because I have dealt with this at length elsewhere.[9] In
general, Africa is very cohesive on voting on African
questions and on the North–South issues in the United
Nations, but is fairly divided on the more traditional
East–West issues. Whether this situation will continue if
the African Group is frustrated in its efforts to obtain
strong moves against South Africa and Portugal and to
obtain representation on the major organs of the United
Nations is not easy to tell. Whether the recent dissolution
of the Casablanca and AMU caucusing groups will encourage greater voting cohesion cannot yet be determined. The impact of the 1963 Addis Ababa Conference
can be seen in the high degree of cohesion of Africa in
UN voting in the Eighteenth Session of the General
Assembly.

What is apparent is that as the African Group increases
in size with the admission of new members it will come
closer and closer to the point where its membership will
constitute one-third-plus-one of the total membership of
the United Nations. If that should occur in the not-too-

distant future, then a solid unified front of African votes
would be in a controlling position on all important
questions in the General Assembly which require a two
thirds majority for passage.

Responsibility

The final point about the role of the African states in the
United Nations must be a consideration of the degree to
which the behavior of these states is responsible. The
actions of states in the United Nations are often characterized as being responsible or irresponsible. While there
is no precise definition of what constitutes responsible
behavior, it might be suggested that, as the term is used
in the United Nations, responsible behavior is behavior
that shows an awareness of political reality. For example,
the African states might use their thirty-five votes to jam
a resolution through the General Assembly that would be
wholly unrealistic because it was not supported by the
states that would be primarily responsible for its implementation or enforcement. In another sense it has to be
recognized that in an international organization where
each state has an equal vote it is possible for recommendations to be taken without a direct relation to the power
of states. Such action is not possible in the Security
Council because the major powers (at least the major
powers as of 1945) can by a negative vote prevent action
that they are not willing to implement. But this is not the
case in the General Assembly, and therefore action in the
General Assembly is judged as responsible if it takes into
account the realities of political power.

On the basis of this sort of a sense of responsibility—an
awareness of the political realities—it might be argued

that the African states tend to exercise a good deal of responsibility in the United Nations. A few examples might be briefly cited to indicate the degree and type of this responsibility. In the Committee of Twenty-Four, the African and Asian states have a majority of sixteen out of the twenty-four possible votes. Invariably the African states have introduced proposals on the elimination of colonialism with regard to some specific area. They have in their introduction of the proposal assured its passage. But their desire, as indicated both in the public discussions and behind the scenes, has been not simply to force the passage of the proposal but to make efforts to accept modifications so that the proposal could achieve as nearly unanimous acceptance as possible. In essence they made overtures for modifications to try to get the support of the United States and the United Kingdom. They were willing to try to weaken their ultimate desires to get the widest support. This process became fairly well established as a routine of negotiation in the Committee of Twenty-Four until about February 1963, when the Soviet Union began to make counterproposals that went much further than the African proposals, further in the direction than the African states would have desired. In a sense this prevented the African states from trying to seek the support of the United States and the United Kingdom, because they would have had a hard time publicly not supporting the more extreme positions of the Soviet Union. For several months this situation prevailed until the African states raised the question of the possible expulsion of South Africa and Portugal from the United Nations. When the first efforts at ouster were made in the I.L.O. Conference, the African states suggested that this principle of expulsion might be applied in the United Nations for states that violate the principles of the Charter. But the Soviet

Union, behind in its financial assessments, is opposed to the concept of expulsion for obvious reasons. The net effect of raising the question of a principle of expulsion forced a withdrawal of the Soviet tactics in the Committee of the Twenty-Four and the African states could again resume their previous tactics of negotiation to try to achieve near-unanimity, rather than to pass resolutions supported by their set majority in the Committee. I would argue that this is evidence of responsible behavior in the United Nations.

Other examples could be cited. Even though they have met with constant frustration until recently in the Security Council, the African states recognize that the only obligatory action that can be taken in the United Nations has to come from the Security Council, where the cards are almost stacked against them. Nonetheless, in every major effort they seriously attempt to have the Security Council consider and to act on their problem. Only when they meet rejection in the Security Council do they turn to the General Assembly. The African states may disagree with the way in which the Secretary General handled the situation in the Congo, but they have defended the Secretary General when other critics of his action used their criticism as a step to attacking the institution of the Secretary General. Some African states may have withdrawn their troops from the Congo, but for the sake of the principle of peace-keeping operations of the United Nations, they have continued to pay their financial obligation for these forces. All of these actions I feel are further evidence of responsibility.

It would be very difficult to come to general conclusions about the impact of African politics on the character and development of the United Nations. Nonetheless, the image that the African states have created in the United Nations, with all its facets, has provided other states and observers with insights into the nature of these new members of the international community. And I suspect that experts on Africa could see deeper implications in all these points of observation that may not be easy for a non-African specialist to discern.

5

THE PRIMACY OF
POLITICAL DEVELOPMENT

HERBERT J. SPIRO

Since publication of *The Politics of the Developing Areas* in 1960 a considerable literature about various aspects of political development has been growing. Much of it has been critical and some of it even polemical—in the sense that scholars have been engaging in what almost deserves the label of a "great debate," putting forth different theories of political development, attacking one another's explanations, and—happily—testing hypotheses. New hypotheses have been built upon partly or wholly discarded old ones, so that one might even speak of a "second generation" of writings in the field.

Here—as in the sub-field of contemporary African politics—there has been little scholarly consensus, an absence of agreement that can be taken as a symptom of the youth, vigor, and good health of this area of study. And if the lack of consensus is understood in this sense, then the same understanding could be transposed to the subject matter of political development itself. In other words, just as the generation of more debate, of wider scope and clearer focus, bears witness to the general health of the

study of political development, so the generation of more
debate, of wider scope and clearer focus within the
developing political systems themselves could be interpreted as testifying to the general good health of their
politics. In fact, the opposite interpretation has more
often been placed upon these phenomena; that is, the
proliferation of issues in the new systems is frequently
described as "dysfunctional" to development, because it is
believed to reduce the consensus needed to sustain development. I consider this approach mistaken, and would
explain its prevalence as flowing largely from the conceptions of politics upon which it is based. These conceptions
either continue the traditional preoccupation with power;
or they relegate politics to a position of secondary or
tertiary importance in the hierarchy of human activities
(after economic, social, and cultural processes); or they
suffer from both these defects.

A perhaps slightly simplified and exaggerated theory of
political development based upon a combination of these
misconceptions would run along the following lines: the
goal of development is to enhance the elite's capacity to
marshal the power of the country for purposes of modernization. From a Western point of view, the desirability of
also achieving "stable democracy" should be added to
this goal. The achievement of stable democracy is directly
dependent upon the degree of the presence or absence of
certain "prerequisites," like wealth, industrialization, ur-
banization, education, and communications.[1] As the preconditions improve, the power capacity of the elite also
grows, though there is no necessary parallel increase in
the chances for stable democracy. In the course of all this,
"development" is taking place primarily in the country's
economy, society, and culture, and only secondarily in its
politics. The very title, *The Politics of the Developing
Areas,* suggests that this is the sequence: development in

the substantive substructure first; then its effects upon or
reflections in politics.

These misconceptions of politics breed a fuzzy, unre-
fined notion of consensus that is injected into some
theories of development, thereby further detracting from
their validity. By relating political development to communications and socialization indices, to the growth of
"empathy," or to such functions as "interest aggregation," the suggestion is made, sometimes implicitly, more
often explicitly, that a high level of "agreement on fundamentals" is an additional prerequisite for successful development. If such consensus is lacking, the argument
seems to say, the elite will find it difficult to mobilize the
society's power on behalf of modernization. Or, even if it
should succeed in this respect, the further goal of moving
toward stable democracy will be thwarted.

These theories reverse the actual sequence of events. In
virtually every historical instance, substantive change in
economy, society, culture, or elsewhere was brought about
by political action. Individuals and groups became aware
of their desire to bring about substantive change and then
took more or less deliberate action to effect it. The
stimulation of this awareness, to be sure, often comes
from "development" in the substantive environment. This
development, in turn, flows from both political and nonpolitical antecedents. For example, the growth and shift
of population is caused by both technological change and
the policies of indigenous or colonial elites. But with the
dawn of awareness of the feasibility of deliberately effect-
ing changes in the substantive environment, this process
of "modernization" is subjected to politics. (Incidentally,
these facts can be taken as another illustration of Bis-
marck's dictum that politics is the art of the possible.) In
a community whose members are unaware of the possibilities of doing something about their common fate,

there is no politics to the extent of this unawareness. The moment, and to the extent, that some members do become aware of the possibility of doing something about their economic welfare, their social structure, their cultural values, or other aspects of their common existence, politics begins—and begins to develop.

Nowadays, in Africa and in other "developing areas," as in the already developed areas for varying periods of time, a high degree of consciousness prevails of the feasibility of shaping the common fate of the community. This does not mean that all changes that do occur are direct products of politics; or that changes effected through politics are (in Merton's phrase) "intended consequences of purposive [political] action"; or that much political action does not also have unanticipated—and unanticipatable—consequences. It is meant to assert that politics *in* the developing areas is in the main not a secondary result of economic, social, cultural, and other substantive development, or of modernization. *What has been studied as the politics of development should instead be studied as the development of politics.*

However, so long as "legitimate physical compulsion" remains the central concern of the comparative study of political development,[2] we may expect that it will continue to be studied as the politics of development. In other words, we will continue to try to improve our understanding of "the impact *on* politics of various factors making for change."[3] This angle of attack will continue to foreshorten our perspective and distort the results of analysis. In such studies, political development will appear only as a secondary effect of other primary changes, and mainly in the form of increases in a ruling group's capacity to apply legitimate physical compulsion, that is, power.

If, however, we think of politics as the process by which a community deals with the common problems that its

members face and recognize, then political development
will appear as an enlargement in the capacity of a
political system to generate new goals and to expand and
improve the formulation, deliberation, and resolution of
issues.[4] The development of politics occurs with increases
in the "network's" capacity to bear a "load" of issues
without either a blowup or a breakdown. The capacity to
exert physical compulsion, legitimate or illegitimate, may,
but need not, increase as a concomitant of this development of politics. But issues can be processed not only
more or less violently, that is, with the use or threat of
force, but also legalistically, ideologically, pragmatically,
or in various combinations of these four principal patho-
logical political styles. Politics may develop in a country
(or other political system) without either enhancement of
its power capacity, or modernization of its socio-economic substructure, or strengthening of its substantive
consensus. On the contrary, each of these changes may
work to the detriment of political development.

The colonial or traditional elites of most new states
were generally much more powerful than their successors
of the immediate post-independence period; but politics
was developed by and eventually under their less powerful
(initially at least) successors. Economic, social, and cultural modernization was either given its crucial push after
politics was generated in the post-independence years, or
else—where the colonial or traditional elites promoted
modernization, as in the Belgian Congo and Ethiopia—
modernization was not accompanied by the development
of politics. The consensus of political stagnation that
generally prevailed in Africa before the beginning of
independence agitation was conducive to neither socio-
economic modernization nor political development.

Increases in power, advances in substantive modernization, and the strengthening of apparent agreement on

fundamentals can all be imposed from above or from the outside, without the growth of politics, either parallel or prior. Failure to recognize this—and, frequently, insistence upon its opposite—accounts for much of the misinterpretation and false prognostication of African politics —within individual states, among them in Africa, and in world politics—to which we have been exposed, with respect to independence movements, the timing of independence, and the politics of independence.

The development of politics in African territories has generally tended to follow one broad pattern, within which several possible variations can be discerned. In the colony, until some time after World War II, there was no significant politics. Administration prevailed in the place of politics; that is, problems were recognized, if at all, for—not by—the indigenous population. The attempts to solve problems came from above and outside. No new goals were invented internally. Consensus prevailed on the propriety, or the legitimacy, of this condition, at least to the extent that no one voiced disagreement.

With the dawn of awareness of the possibility of working toward independence on the part of the leaders of incipient movements, this consensus is destroyed and one central issue, the issue of independence, is introduced into the larger political system, of which the colonial administration until then had been the "weightier part." While destroying the old consensus of the larger system, introduction of this issue at the same time also lays the foundation for a new consensus, on the goal of independence, among the politically conscious African population. Though the colonial administration controls a monopoly of the means of legitimate compulsion, and the independence movement has very little physical force at its disposal, the latter wins. Its leadership then tries to carry forward into the beginnings of statehood the con-

sensus on the already achieved goal, by transferring this
agreement to new goals, usually economic, social, and
cultural modernization and the achievement of wider, and
eventually Pan-African, associations. To varying degrees,
there follows failure of these efforts to transfer the old
consensus to newly adopted, and sometimes newly invented, goals. Issues are formulated concerning the goals,
their desirability, and the priority in which they should
be pursued, and the policies and the constitutional framework best suited for achieving them. With the proliferation of issues, the development of politics begins to get
into high gear.

The development of politics naturally takes on as many
different forms as there are political systems. The differences cannot be satisfactorily described, much less explained, by focusing on formal institutions, on functions
linked with the exercise of power, or on nonpolitical
modernization. On the other hand, changes in capacity to
process issues and changes in political style do seem to me
promising approaches to description, classification, comparison, and explanation.

We might ask, for example, what has been the trend in
the formulation and deliberation of issues, and of what
types of issues, in Nigeria, or the Congo, or Malawi, over
a certain period of time? Has there been a steady increase
in issues? If so, I would suggest this fact by itself is more
significant than the institutional framework within and by
which the issues were generated and processed. In other
words, we learn more about political development as the
development of politics from an increase in the generation
of issues than from a decrease in the organizations (like
political parties) that participate in this processing. An
increase in issues indicates greater inventiveness of goals
and greater awareness of the possibilities of politics. The

establishment of a "mass party regime," to use Professor Moore's term, tells us very little by itself.

Similarly, the particular mixture of legalism, pragmatism, ideologism, and violence in the treatment of issues tells us more about the more enduring patterns of politics, especially in the "developing countries" whose fluidity is forever stressed by observers, than an examination of the background and origins of any group of contemporary power-holders. How do politicians seek to persuade others and themselves of the propriety of the stand they are taking on particular issues—in terms of their capacity to compel compliance by police or mob action; of the dictates of an ideology of anti-neocolonialism or Pan-Africanism; of the provisions of national or international constitutions; of the immediate material benefits to be derived from the policy under debate? What profile of political style emerges from the comparison of the treatment in different political systems of similar issues—like labor policy or land reform, adherence to the Organization of African Unity, or participation in the United Nations' Congo operation?

I think questions like these are likely to yield more useful answers than questions based upon the conceptions of politics criticized above. If we compared the power potential or the power locus of two mass party regimes, we would probably find few differences susceptible to explanation or helpful in forecasting. If we compared the performance of such functions as political socialization and recruitment, interest articulation, interest aggregation, and political communication,[5] chances are again that we would end up in the *cul de sac* of misclassification —largely because these functions, far from being universals of political systems in their varying types and different degrees of differentiation, are simple transfers from certain Western prototypes (for example, interest groups articulate and political parties aggregate interests in the United States and Great Britain, but not in France before the Fifth Republic). Implied in this approach is the dual assumption or expectation that the African political systems are developing toward the present condition of these Western models, and that they will have to pass through the same stages of development, in the same sequence, which characterized the development of the United States "as a new nation."[6] This expectation has not been borne out in the recent past, and it is unlikely to be fulfilled in the future.[7]

The prevailing approaches to the study of the politics of development thus prejudge the cases under scrutiny. The changed focus on the development of politics that I am proposing is meant to eliminate this United States-centered bias. Instead of asking to what extent and at what rate politics in the new systems is emulating the United States model, I am asking (in a comparative way) how politics is developing. The merit of this approach, as I see it, comes mainly from the more nearly universal and basic conception of politics upon which it rests: politics is the process by which a community deals with the issues arising out of its common problems. The basic functions of politics, after the pre-political recognition of problems, are the formulation of issues, the deliberation of issues, the resolution of issues, and the solution of the problems that gave rise to issues in the first of these four "phases."

The comparative study of political development by this approach suggests, in Africa and elsewhere, four major patterns which occur in a variety of combinations. After the initial generation of the one great issue of independence and the attainment of this goal, described above, the leadership makes an effort to transfer the consensus of the independence movement to newer goals, including modernization. The main patterns of development that follow can be described as the crumbling of consensus, procedural routinization, enforced consensus, and the development of politics.

1. *Crumbling consensus.* The leadership fails in its efforts to transfer the previous agreement on the desirability of independence to the goals it now considers most important. This often happens because neither leaders nor followers were given sufficient experience with politics under colonial administration or in their own traditional societies. The earlier goal of independence was seen as a substantive goal. The earlier consensus, therefore, had relatively little procedural content. The independence struggle was carried on and won without an established procedural framework, that is, without "rules of the game."

Consensus may crumble with two major types of results, in different possible combinations:

a. Substantive interests predominate, like tribal or other ethnic groups, religious denominations, economic classes, institutional groups including the military. In this case, violence is probable, and the breakup of the political system is possible.

b. No interests are "articulated," no goals—and especially no new goals—are formulated. The system returns to its previous stagnation, to the unconscious consensus on the *status quo ante*. In Latin America, the failure to articulate new interests was combined with the predominance of two or three pre-independence substantive interests, like the Church, the big landowners, and the inarticulate Indians. The cleavages between these substantive interests have provided the ruts in which the politics of most Latin American systems have been revolving.

2. *Procedural routinization.* The leadership continues to act out mechanically certain political or administrative

procedures which it learned to copy from the colonial rulers or its own traditional forebears. These procedures are adopted *in toto* without being adapted to the newly independent system and its new needs. For example, administrative procedures are uselessly routinized when methods designed for maintaining colonial control over a politically unaware population are transferred to the new government which is, in some way, based upon popular consent. Parliamentary procedure is routinized when an opposition party formally opposes every measure introduced by the government without regard to the substantive interests involved, simply because it wants to perform the role of the parliamentary opposition as it understands that role in the Westminster model. Procedural routinization tends to interfere with substantive development and to discourage experimentation with procedures better suited to the new needs and to the popular experience (if any) with politics at lower levels, both local and associational.

3. *Enforced consensus.* The leaders who rode into power acrest the independence movement, upon discovering that achievement of its goal has removed their program and their *raison d'être,* impose an artificial consensus upon the society. The objects of this consensus may include the greatness of the leader, the evils of a neighboring state, the vices of neocolonialism, and the benefits of the modernization plan. Artificial consensus is often imposed after the first signs that the earlier natural consensus is beginning to crumble. Where enforced consensus is dedicated to a single substantive goal, the system is moving toward "totalitarianism."[8]

4. *The development of politics.* Consensus on the goal of independence is successfully transferred to an evolving balance of substantive and procedural concerns, including modernization of economy, society, and culture *and* de-

velopment of a political system that combines stability
with flexibility, efficiency with effectiveness. As old goals
are approached, new goals are invented. The leaders
succeed in eliciting popular understanding of and support
for these new goals. The politically interested population
is given experience with political procedures applied to
substantive problems that are of importance to this population at lower levels. The capacity of the system to carry
loads of issues constantly increases. Its style develops in
dynamic equilibrium.

The four preceding chapters have shown the great
variety of combinations in which these basic patterns of
political development are being followed in Africa. It may
be useful, in conclusion, to apply this approach to the
study of political development by returning to some of the
questions raised in my Introduction.

I agree with Professor Bustin's diagnosis of the ills of
the Congo: the country suffers from too little politics. The
dearth of politics, moreover, cannot be explained in terms
of a comparative shortage of political power or a relatively low level of economic and social modernization.
The Force Publique was the largest and strongest military
force turned over to a new African state by its departing
colonial administration. And the substantial modern sector of the economy was as far advanced as, and perhaps
more important than, its counterparts in any other African colony, with the possible exception of Southern Rhodesia.

The failure of a Congolese independence movement to
develop as early as in neighboring colonies, like the
Rhodesias or Tanganyika, can be explained partly in
terms of the better nonpolitical opportunities for advance-
ment offered to potential Congolese political leaders by
the Belgian administration. This, in turn, was related to
that administration's explicitly anti-political philosophy.

Since no independence movement existed at the time when
Belgium lost its "will to govern" the Congo, an independence movement almost had to be invented. Patrice Lumumba came closest to creating one, but his start was too
late and Belgian or Belgian-sponsored opposition was too
strong to enable him to build up sufficient consensus on
the goal of independence to transfer this consensus to the
period after June 30, 1960.

By this time, no resilient, flexible network for the
processing of problems had been brought into being. By
contrast with neighboring territories, in the Congo the
ablest Africans had not been able to go into politics even
as a part-time vocation. The shortage of politicians contributed, along with various outside influences, to the
dearth of politics. As a result, while administration often
simply ceased, parliamentary politics—as long as it lasted
—became simultaneously less effective and more routinized. Whenever Parliament seemed to be threatening to
address itself to the country's substantive problems, the
President and Prime Minister managed to avert the
threat, until the final dismissal and dissolution of Parliament. The Congo must be the only African ex-colony
where no country-wide elections or referenda were held
for four years after the achievement of independence.

Because no consensus on the desirability of independence had ever been generated, no consensus could
crumble. The denial of influence on the country's substantive problems to parliamentarians led to some procedural
routinization, which remained without long-run consequences because of the peripheral role of the Parliament
and the low authority attaching to the Belgian parliamentary procedures involved. Since the death of Lumumba, no politician has attempted to create a natural
consensus, much less to enforce an imposed consensus.
Despite varying degrees of economic, educational, and

technical growth, derived largely from outside assistance, politics developed very little in the years between 1960 and 1964.

In Nigeria, by contrast, the capacity of the political system to recognize and process problems and issues has been constantly expanding. The proportion of the population interested and participating in politics has been growing. Despite the high prestige of British parliamentary and administrative procedures and the consequent temptation to routinize these, procedures have in fact been kept flexible in a symbiotic way that may have begun to blend British with indigenous procedures. Consensus on independence, which was strong at least in the south, has been transferred fairly successfully to new evolving goals, including modernization, so that the leadership has not found it necessary to attempt the imposition of an artificial agreement about any single substantive goal.

Accepting Professor Bretton's description of politics in the southern regions, I would draw rather different conclusions from the facts that he observed. Instead of seeing the beginnings of a totalitarian apparatus, I see the beginnings of political development. Totalitarianism has always aimed at the abolition of politics in order to harness the society totally to pursuit of one substantive goal, like racial mastery or proletarian rule. No such single goal has been advanced in Nigeria—or even in Ghana, for that matter. On the contrary, I interpret the facts presented by Professor Bretton to show a dynamic balance between the various substantive and procedural goals that are being pursued in Nigerian politics, and I expect this moving equilibrium to enable Nigeria to improve its political system with relatively little violence, ideologism, or legalism. Although I agree with his criticism of David Apter's expectation of the transfer of

British institutions and procedures to Africa, I would turn the same critique against Professor Bretton's own analysis of Nigerian politics, because it uses criteria originally derived from the very Western "political thought and practice" which is in fact not being transferred. Instead, the comparatively pragmatic style of traditionally consensual sub-systems is being applied to initially and superficially British-type institutions. Politics proceeds through face-to-face contacts and personal channels of communications. Formal lines of command or influence are disregarded. And although he frequently found ideological language, Professor Bretton found no ideological motivation.

All of these trends could be taken as indices of the successful development of politics. Professor Bretton, however, brings out their negative aspects, including the difficulty of rational planning. Here he appears to agree with Professor Moore, according to whom the price of the primacy of politics, which is proclaimed by all the mass party regimes, is a corrosive anti-intellectualism inimical to development. I am tempted to describe this critical attitude as evincing a corrosive intellectualism that occasionally characterizes political scientists and technocrats working on and in not only African contexts. They consider modernization or, say, European unification, as more valuable than the development of politics, and would prefer to have some "rational" blueprint put into effect with—to be sure—popular approval elicited by a competitive party system.

This approach seems to me to suffer from misidentification of familiar American and British institutions with allegedly universal political functions. In the instances cited, political parties are probably identified with the functions of representation and competition, but the questions are not asked: Representation of what? Competition for what purpose? My answer would be, for the formulation and deliberation of issues. Other answers are possible, but most of them suggest that, where strong consensus prevails, or where no realistic alternative goals or policies are available, the artificial concoction of issues would be a sign of procedural routinization. And where strong disagreement prevails and realistic alternatives are being advanced, it may be possible to carry on deliberation just as well as, or better and even more competitively, within one political movement than between two or more political parties. This is what Professor Moore seems to have in mind when he gives as one alternative for the future of mass party regimes the maintenance of mass loyalties through perpetual renewal. This course of events roughly corresponds to the fourth pattern of development I suggested above, namely the development of politics.

To the extent that they foreclose the possibility of vigorous deliberation within a mass party movement, Professors Bretton and Moore imply a denial of the primacy of politics and of political development. They also lead us to infer that the logic of their criticism derives from, and circularly leads back to, the expectation of the re-enactment in Africa of Western patterns of development destined to end in the reproduction of Western institutions, including the sovereign national state as the most comprehensive and "final" political entity. Conversely, according to Professor Moore, inadequate national representation suggests unsatisfactory or unsuccessful development.

Here Professor Hovet's study of the behavior of Africa's "national" representatives at the United Nations serves as a useful antidote, for three major and related reasons: the unexpectedly high degree of voting cohesion that the African members of the United Nations have been able to demonstrate, the progress they are making toward continental political unity, and the procedures used by African politicians to further both voting cohesion and political unity. To begin with, this behavior suggests that "national integration," in the conventional meaning of the term, is not an important goal of most leadership groups in African states. Consequently, outside analysts like ourselves are making a mistake in using national integration as a criterion for evaluating the performance of the new political systems or their leaders. Those states whose leaders have been described as most "nationalistic" are also the ones who have been most active in promoting various types of Pan-Africanism. This fact has often been explained as an indication of the probability of totalitarianism, for example, by making false analogies between an Nkrumah and a Hitler and the links between their domestic policies and foreign ambitions. These analogies overlook, among many other differences, that between Hitler's Pan-Germanism (or Pan-Aryanism) and the various African leaders' Pan-Africanism: Nkrumah is not a Pan-Ghanaian, Lumumba was not a Pan-Congolese, Dr. Banda is not a Pan-Malawian. Each in his different way is a Pan-African. Each is not only willing, but in different respects eager to skip over certain stages, or at least sub-stages, through which the older national states did pass on their road to national integration and political maturity.

To this an objection is frequently raised that stresses the adjective *different*, used repeatedly above. Pan-Africanism, according to this critical argument, is merely a phrase which means too many different things to too many African leaders to have any operative effectiveness. The remarkable fact, however, is the extent to which these loudly stated differences have been overcome, both in voting at the United Nations and in building Pan-African institutions. The differences between various approaches toward achieving Pan-African unity have been proclaimed so loudly that outside observers repeatedly pronounced them irreconcilable, as they did, for example, during the height of the "split," then apparently institutionalized, between the Casablanca and AMU "blocs." In the face of these outside estimates, the very convening of the Addis Ababa conference of May 1963 was an achievement by itself, regardless of any enduring effects that it may have had. How can this steady progress toward unity be explained?

To begin with, all the colonial independence movements were committed to some form of Pan-Africanism as an integral concomitant of the goal of independence itself. And the two states that had already been members of the League of Nations, Liberia and Ethiopia, successfully tried to jump on the Pan-African bandwagon. The goal of Pan-African association and, ultimately, unity had, in other words, been popularized from the very beginnings of political development, at the dawn of the awareness of the possibilities of political action.

This still calls for an explanation of the partial and progressive reconciliation between apparently antagonistic visions of Pan-Africanism. Why, for example, did the Casablanca and the Monrovia groups of states agree to ignore their obvious if temporary substantive differences for the sake of cooperation in the United Nations and in Africa? The most promising approach to an answer should, I think, focus on the consensual character of many—probably most—traditional African societies. Anthropological studies cast light on this, as do the first theoretical reflections upon the "African way of life" in which Africans themselves have recently engaged. Objective and subjective observers frequently agree in emphasizing the prevalence of consensus—however vaguely perceived or defined—and the high value placed upon consensus, in both traditional societies and now in, and among, the new states of Africa. Since there are in fact many substantive disagreements at all levels, especially in the contemporary polities, the consensus must be principally upon the procedures by means of which these disagreements are handled. Without some such profound procedural consensus it should have been impossible, for example, for African diplomats at the United Nations to achieve the high degree of cohesion that Professor Hovet describes, especially in view of their lack of parliamentary and diplomatic experience, which he also stresses.

I see here a promising field for further research: the communal, judicial, and more properly "political" procedures used in various African pre-modern societies, and their reflection in, or adaptation to the needs of, contemporary politics within Africa and between Africa and the rest of the world. Perhaps such research would offer one explanation for the apparent skill of many Africans in the use of old and development of new procedures for the many levels of politics which they are trying to integrate with one another, as well as an explanation for the delight they take in politics.

Even if the development of politics within Africa were less important and less intrinsically interesting than it appears at least to those who, like the contributors to this book, have made it one of their special fields of study, then the contribution of Africa to world politics, especially at the United Nations, would still merit thorough study. If Professor Hovet is right, and I believe he is, African diplomats are making creative, innovative contributions to United Nations procedure. And the UN as the focal point of world politics is itself ideally suited for a study of the development of politics. It was founded upon substantive consensus among the victorious powers of

World War II. The founding consensus crumbled soon
after victory, to be replaced by the bickering of the Cold
War. Substantive interests predominated, violence repeatedly broke out, and the breakup of the system seemed
imminent more than once. These developments were accompanied or followed by both procedural routinization
in the United Nations and attempts to impose an artificial
consensus within each of the two opposing blocs. All
along, however, and increasingly so in recent years,
politics of a more balanced style has been developing in
the United Nations, through the creation of new substantive goals and the invention of new procedures. Africans
have made helpful contributions to this conversion of the
politics of development in the United Nations into the
development of the politics of the United Nations. These
contributions constitute another demonstration of the
primacy of politics in Africa.

APPENDIX

POLITICAL INFLUENCE IN
SOUTHERN NIGERIA:
METHODS USED IN
THE SURVEY

❦

HENRY L. BRETTON

The sample consisted of 95 persons interviewed in the following towns, in the order given: Abeokuta (West); Enugu, Umuahia, Aba, Port Harcourt, Owerri, and Onitsha (East); Warri and Benin (Mid-West); Akure and Ibadan (West). Interviews were conducted between June 22 and August 26, 1963. The following procedures were used to arrive at the interview sample:

I asked people familiar with various phases of government and politics in several Nigerian federal ministries, in several agencies identified with the United States Mission to Nigeria, and in a private foundation to suggest names of influential persons throughout the areas to be visited. Qualifications asked for were actual or potential ability to influence critical socio-economic decisions, other outstanding leadership capabilities, or unusual familiarity with the influence structure in a given region or municipality. This first step produced a sizable list of

contacts in all areas on the itinerary. It also confirmed a
previous impression that the weight of influence appeared
to be applied mainly in the towns and cities. As I reached
a locality, I visited first the person on the list who had
been designated as most influential. The interview with
him yielded at least five additional nominations reflecting
his concept of a segment or segments of the regional and
local influence structures. Names of groups believed to be
influential were also obtained. I followed up nominations
selectively with a view to fairly equitable distribution
among the major socio-metric clusters (tribal segments,
traditional rulers, government officials, leaders and managers of major political parties and interest groups,
administrators, professionals, members of the clergy,
businessmen and traders, both men and women). The
logistics of travel and scheduling did of course dictate
certain omissions or adjustments. One major group was
deliberately left out: federal Cabinet members and regional Premiers as well as most regional Cabinet members were not included in the sample. Although clearly in
positions of influence, power, and prestige, members of
this group tend to be relatively inaccessible and previous
experience has shown that they are given, of necessity, to
vague generalizations concerning politically sensitive subjects. Members of this group promised a relatively low
yield of useful information in terms of man-hours spent.

I initially determined suitable subjects for interview by
referring to the criteria for influence status upon which
the questionnaire itself (see pages 186–188) was based.
Subsequent determination of suitability was based on the
same criteria. To avoid restricting the sample to the qualifications of reputation alone, additional tests of influence
potential and performance were applied, including questions designed to produce concrete evidence of influence
wielded and results obtained.

THE INTERVIEW PATTERN: GENERALIZED

Initial Informant

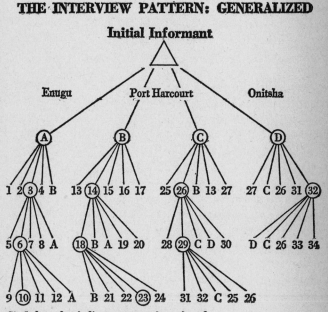

Circled number indicates persons interviewed.

In Enugu, respondent *A* was interviewed because he had been nominated by the initial informant; respondent *3* was selected because he had been nominated by *A* and because he represented the only member of his particular socio-metric cluster who was available. Respondents *6* and *10* were selected further to assure equitable representation of major socio-metric clusters in the sample. Frequently, the same person was nominated by several respondents, thus providing a certain confirmation of influence status.

Traditional patterns of behavior in Africa suggested that channels of influence in the area under investigation are multi-dimensional, that is, few if any influence-wielders apply their influence only at one level and only in a restricted circle. Thus, by casting a wide net, with checks built into the questionnaire, and a random departure from patterns suggested in the interviews, I felt that a representative sample of key wielders of influence could be obtained with a high degree of probability that the names emerging from the interviews would indeed represent the influence elite in Southern Nigeria, and the associational and group ties indicated in the responses would indeed reflect the influence structure.[1]

The questionnaire was designed to produce a matrix of information reflecting a variety of aspects of the respondent's public role. The major points looked for were his own perception of his role and influence status as a means of verifying his leadership function and his recall of recent contacts with persons who in his view were "important" persons in the political influence context. This was to provide further identification of the respondent's position and role in the influence structure. Further verification of his own influence function was sought by questions inviting recall of major positions held by him in public and private spheres. To obtain additional clues about sources of influence in the area, he was asked for his perception of the locus of authoritative decision-making on critical issues. Additional data on the web of influence were sought by questions about the respondent's contacts with constituents, friends, and neighbors, about the type of advice rendered by him, if any, and by questions requesting recall of instances where the respondent obtained advice and guidance from persons whom he regarded as superior to himself in social status and influence. I was interested in the respondent's recall of methods employed by him to gauge the state of public opinion on a given issue, or, in general, I aimed at information on the leader–public relationship. His recall of the five most influential groups in the area provided additional bases for the selection of interview targets. To obtain information on latent aspects of the respondent's political perception regarding his own role and that of others, he was asked to recall groups and persons in the area who tended to oppose him or the positions taken by him. Specific recommendations for additional interview targets were obtained by request for the names and addresses of "the five most influential persons" at the regional or local levels. As mentioned earlier, this was followed up with a request for concrete supporting evidence. A final attempt was made to bring out latent impressions by a request for recall of a recent controversy in the area and of the names of persons who had played leading roles for and against the position taken by the respondent himself. At the beginning, a question was asked to clarify the respondent's own concept of influence and, at the end, a question about his educational background. Certain biographical data were also obtained because of the established unreliability of published sources. There is no doubt in my mind that the questionnaire could be improved for a second survey. I also have no doubt that numerous errors were made and wrong stimuli applied; in other words, no suggestion of perfection should be inferred. I believe, however, that the questionnaire, applied in depth as it were, produced a good profile of the influence structure in the area and useful data concerning the flow of influence and the relevant channels of communication.

It is possible that the data collected lend themselves to statistical analysis. But I felt that the data should first be analyzed in the raw, uncoded state, partly because I believed that coding to facilitate statistical analysis would grossly distort the data, and would obscure, and possibly wipe out, significant variations and nuances. Ultimately, data from this study should be correlated with materials gathered on previous surveys and materials obtained from published sources, such as newspapers. Of special interest for further study should be an analysis of the responses regarding the role of traditional rulers, and the evident dichotomy between stated and actual aims of political parties and between their programmatic and pragmatic—perhaps opportunistic—orientations. I am reminded of Lucian Pye's observation that "political parties in non-Western societies tend to take on a world view and represent a way of life."[2] Current observations on the role of the tribe and other groups in "nation-building" also should be tested specifically in the light of relevant responses in the present survey.

A few words are in order concerning the utility of research focused only on key role-players in the political influence structure without simultaneous identification and study of all other conceivable factors bearing on the influence complex. I suggest that such a study should be left to detailed, micro-research and should be restricted to a relatively narrow, hence more controllable geographic area. Moreover, it is entirely possible that one ends up, in such extended study, with extremely elusive, indistinct, rather nebulous aggregates of social relationships which may or may not have a significant bearing on political influence.

Of course, numerous responses indicate the existence of what may be called sub-systems of political influence. No doubt some kind of influence is exerted throughout all channels of social communication, all the way down to the individual family unit. Also, political bargaining takes place at all levels and invariably triggers a great variety of forms of influence; for example, to survive politically, regional party headquarters must inevitably take into account diverse and competing claims of a great variety of groups of actual or potential supporters at all levels. Although this "wheel within wheel" type of influence is of significance in some socio-political contexts, I would suggest that it lacks enough identifiable substance to be of value here. In that connection, French and Raven's observation may be relevant:

The concept of power has the conceptual property of potentiality; but it seems useful to restrict this potential influence to more or less enduring power relations between O and P by excluding from the definition of power those cases where the potential influence is so momentary or so changing that it cannot be predicted from the existing relationship. Power is a useful concept for describing social structure only if it has a certain stability over time; it is useless if every momentary social stimulus is viewed as actualizing social power.[3]

It might be added that the power increment at the disposal of a regional organizational headquarters of a political party is so great that it can afford to ignore, or materially reduce in importance, any countervailing influences emanating from lesser or sub-groups, groups which must operate without adequate leadership or material resources. While it would seem that the regional head-quarters will make an effort, in the ordinary course of political operations, to adjust to conflicting demands from local sub-groups, within or outside the party, responses indicated that a showdown finds the regional leadership endowed with the requisite increment of power to prevail in a contest of wills. Thus I am suggesting that in the Nigerian setting, perhaps everywhere in developing socie-ties—and in ordinary circumstances—influence capabili-ties at the disposal of low-level sub-groups are so small, and their capabilities of maximization of their limited power potential so low, that their individual or collective impact on the political influence structure is negligible, or at best cumulative.

METHODOLOGICAL AND PROCEDURAL
PROBLEMS ENCOUNTERED

To be rendered meaningful to the majority of the po-tential respondents, questions had to be tested in a few preliminary interviews. These tests established that inter-views of this type, on sensitive points with sensitive respondents, were best conducted by a person equipped with the knowledge, background, and command of subject matter to make any necessary on-the-spot adjustments for a variety of purposes. Field research in political science in Africa is not yet sufficiently advanced to foresee all contingencies.

On occasion, verbal comprehension tests had to be applied to determine the extent to which a respondent understood the language and intent of the questionnaire. Perhaps this should have been done in all cases, but time did not permit. Frequently, several formulations of the questions had to be tried before a satisfactory degree of comprehension was attained. An effort was made to record these formulations along with the answers.

With regard to a question on the locus of decision-making, I realized halfway through the interview period that respondents would answer more meaningfully if decision-making was broken down into specific, familiar, functional areas (political, governmental, religious, cultural). Similarly, decision-makers generally seem to be known by their functional or vocational association.

A great deal of time was consumed in obtaining correct spelling of names. Respondents in that part of the world evidence great difficulty in providing correct spelling of the names of even their closest friends and associates, especially if the latter are of different tribal origins.[4]

Selective recall was of course a major source of distortion. In the main, respondents recall only what they want or find convenient to recall; they will remember their most recent brush with a person of influence potential, instead of a person considerably more influential but momentarily forgotten. To correct this, at least in part, interviews were conducted in depth to detect blocks and areas of sensitivity, and to uncover relevant but forgotten communication links.

Many respondents, probably largely because of their British-influenced training, viewed politics, political influence, and related terms rather formalistically, strictly within the legal-constitutional or political-party contexts. These people had to be informed of the much broader concept underlying the present project. However, it should be noted that some respondents proved to be quite sophisticated in this regard. Several requested prior submission of a written questionnaire. This request was not honored, for in all probability answers would have been the combined products of advisers.

Respondents were asked to think of persons who "could

get things done with regard to public policy, public programs, public affairs, if they set their minds to it." In response, nominations, of course, were made in a highly subjective manner, reflecting different concepts of a great variety of sources of power and influence. Influence was variously perceived as related to "respectability," "notoriety," "ability to command attention," "education," "moral conduct," "royal birth," "chieftaincy status," "cabinet status," or "wealth." Influence also was perceived as based on ability to reward and to punish, on legitimacy, on expertness, skill, and knowledge. Legitimacy appeared to be most readily thought of as a source of influence. Consequently, traditional rulers were nominated with greater consistency than other categories. However, with few exceptions, neither the rulers themselves—many of whom sought to impress the interviewer with a sense of importance attached to traditional rule— nor secular persons nominating them, could, when pressed, produce concrete evidence of influence-wielding in the sense here employed.[5]

With regard to each interview, it was only in the context of all answers to the questionnaire that the degree of relevance of specific replies to the study of political influence could be ascertained.

In many instances, depending on the respondent's preference among the several sources of influence and power, groups were named as most influential which, upon cross-check, appeared to be of dubious influence potential. Thus, in the Eastern Region, the Ibo State Union was regularly named, but the nomination withdrawn or highly qualified as soon as a follow-up question sought to extract concrete illustrations. Catholics, religious groups in general, some secret societies such as the Ogbonis, trade unions, and market women, were readily nominated for prime influence status without any supporting evidence.

TABLE I

Identification of Respondents by Primary Occupation

		East	West	Mid-West
I. Ministers Commissioners Board Chairmen	Fed.	—	—	—
	Reg.	1	1	—
II. Politicians	Party Official	1	5	—
	Representative	3	—	1
III. Civil Servants	Fed.	—	—	1
	Reg.	—	4	—
	Loc.	2	3	—
IV. Traditional Rulers		2	7	1
V. Professionals	Doctor	2	2	1
	Lawyer	3	9	—
	Press	4	2	2
VI. Professionals	Teacher	—	1	1
	Principal	2	2	—
VII. Commercial (businessmen, financiers, traders)		12	3	3
VIII. Religious	Clerical	1	2	—
	Lay	—	1	—
IX. Traditional Office Holders		—	—	—
X. Traders		2	2	—
XI. Women Leaders		2	—	—
XII. Trade Union and Cooperative		3	—	—
		—	—	—
TOTAL		40*	44†	11‡ (1 not defined)

* 7 of the respondents were among those nominated by other respondents more than 3 times for leading influence roles.
† 12 of the respondents were among those nominated by other respondents more than 3 times for leading influence roles.
‡ 2 of the respondents were among those nominated by other respondents more than 3 times for leading influence roles.

TABLE II

Grouping of Persons Nominated (More than 3 Times) for Leading Influence Role by Primary Occupation and Source of Influence*

		East		West		Mid-West	
		Occupation	Source of Infl.	Occupation	Source of Infl.	Occupation	Source of Infl.
I. Ministers							
Commissioners	{ Fed.	5	4	3	3	1	1
Board Chairmen	{ Reg.	2	4	5	5	2	2
II. Politicians							
Party Official		5	1	1	3	2	2
Representative	{ Fed.	—	1	1	1	—	—
	{ Reg.	—	3	1	3	—	—
	{ Loc.	—	2	—	2	—	—
III. Civil Servants	{ Fed.	—	—	—	—	—	—
	{ Reg.	1	1	—	—	—	—
	{ Loc.	—	—	1	1	—	—

	1	2	3	4	5	6
IV. Traditional Rulers	2	2	9	8	—	—
V. Professionals — Doctor	—	—	4	1	—	—
V. Professionals — Lawyer	—	—	—	—	—	—
V. Professionals — Press, Radio	—	—	—	—	—	—
VI. Professionals — Teacher	2	1	1	1	—	—
VI. Professionals — Principal	4	—	1	—	—	—
VII. Commercial	3	3	—	—	—	—
VIII. Religious — Clerical	—	2	1	—	—	—
VIII. Religious — Lay	1	1	—	—	—	—
IX. Traditional Office Holders	—	—	1	—	—	—
X. Traders	1	—	—	—	—	—
XI. Women Leaders	—	1	—	—	—	—
XII. Trade Union and Cooperative — Labor	—	—	—	—	—	—
XII. Trade Union and Cooperative — Coop.	—	—	—	—	—	—
TOTAL	25	25	28	28	5	5

* In all, respondents nominated close to 300 influentials. The Sources of Influences are estimated; they refer to the social group or occupational category from which power is most probably derived.

In those instances, respondents seemed to accept reputational qualifications. When pressed, they indicated that the Ibo State Union was influential only in "cultural" respects, religious groups only in "educational" respects, market women only in commercial respects and with regard to voting, and trade unions only with regard to "technical" aspects of labor affairs and then only within narrow compartmental boundaries.

Many respondents failed to mention federal or regional ministers. This may have been because one question specified that what was wanted was "not only big names but names of persons who get things done in the Region if they set their minds to it." It is possible that most federal ministers (except for politicians like Chief Festus Okotie-Eboh, Olu Akinfosile, and T. O. S. Benson) do not as a rule exercise direct influence in the regions outside their own constituencies.

Two rather basic points emerge from this discussion of methodological and procedural problems. First, it is possible to conduct meaningful interviews in an area such as Southern Nigeria and data of some value can be obtained provided the interview addresses itself to subject matter within the range of personal knowledge of the respondent. Second, considerable doubt must be cast upon theoretical and other summary discussions of African political affairs where these are derived primarily by research methods short of close, reasonably controlled, direct observation of actual inter-person and/or inter-group relations viewed in behavioral rather than structural or symbolic terms. The latter methods, highly popular in the West, tend to prejudge and thus distort the findings, precluding, unless supplemented by other methods, significant discoveries and breakthroughs. Particularly dysfunctional in that regard is the tendency of some theorists to rely heavily on discussions of African politics based on evidence of dubious value, such as *Who's Who*, newspaper accounts, autobiographical and largely propagandistic statements of leaders, and electoral manifestos.

As is well known, one of the major problems confronting the researcher in political science, economics, sociology, and anthropology is to develop a sense of evidence similar to that developed by natural scientists. The Africanist's major problem in that regard, as I see it, stems mainly from operational (financial and political) difficulties which separate the researcher from his subject. Under adverse conditions, the least the Africanist can do is to develop his critical faculties and to be more cautious, perhaps more responsible and selective with regard to the sources he employs and quotes.

Questionnaire

Presentation of calling card.

Presentation of copy of my *Power and Stability in Nigeria* for inspection.

Presentation of a letter of introduction from the University of Michigan.

Brief explanation of purpose: the need for more reliable data on a country we want to assist.

1. What does the word "influence" mean to you? What is an influential person?
2. You have been designated a very important person, a leading personality.
   a. Have you done anything recently, in particular in the way of support of public issues, proposals; have you advanced any public proposal, for public improvement?

    b. Are you ever directly consulted, in person, and directly, by individual Ministers or other Government officials?

        (1) By whom?

        (2) On what subject and what are you asked to do?

    c. Are you now a member of any organization, public or private, any agency, board, committee, or commission?

        (1) Please be specific

        (2) What is your particular function in _____?

3. Who, in your opinion, makes important decisions in your area and in the Region—decisions concerning the public as a whole?

        (1) In the Region

        (2) Locally

4. Ordinarily, in the normal course of events, people turn to you for advice and guidance on matters of public interest.

        (1) What type of people are those—what groups, what people?

        (2) What type of advice do you normally give?

5. Suppose that you feel you are inadequately informed on some public issue that has come to your attention, some public controversy perhaps, or a bill before parliament.

        (1) To whom do you normally turn for advice?

        (2) Do you use any other source of information on matters of public policy?

6. When you wish to inform yourself of what the state of public opinion is on a given issue or controversy, how do you go about finding out?

7. Would you please name the five social, economic, or political groups which in your personal opinion are most influential in this Region, that is, which, if their leaders set their minds to it, can get what they want?

    (1) What makes that group so influential? (Select a group.)

    (2) How is that influence related to the way people make their living?

8. Which group in your area tends to oppose things you are in favor of? I do not mean that the group is against you personally, only that it tends to oppose what you stand for.

9. Would you please give me the names of the people who in your opinion are most influential in this Region, not counting the Premier? I am not so much interested in big names as in people who get things done.

    (1) What is the basis of _____'s influence?

10. Can you recall a controversy concerning a public matter which occurred in your community within recent months?

    (1) Who were the people who played leading roles in favor of the position you took?

    (2) Who was against the way you wanted things done?

11. Would you please give me details concerning your education?

NOTES

Introduction

1. See Seymour Martin Lipset, "Some Social Requisites of Democracy: Economic Development and Political Legitimacy," *American Political Science Review*, LIII (1959), 69–105; and Harry Eckstein, *A Theory of Stable Democracy* (1960).
2. Henry L. Bretton, "Political Thought and Practice in Ghana," *American Political Science Review*, LII (1958), 48.
3. See I. William Zartman, *The Sahara—Bridge or Barrier?* (*International Conciliation*: 541, 1963).

1. *The Quest for Political Stability in the Congo:* Soldiers, Bureaucrats and Politicians

1. Cited by E. H. Carr, in *Socialism in One Country*, Vol. 5 of *History of Soviet Russia* (1950–   ), p. 131.
2. S. N. Eisenstadt, "Initial Institutional Patterns of Modernization," *Civilisations*, 4 (1962), 465.
3. These are, incidentally, the major criteria used by international law concerning the recognition of states—or of colonial rule.
4. P. Selznick, *The Organizational Weapon, A Study of Bolshevik Strategy and Tactics* (1957); quoted by David E. Apter and Carl G. Rosberg, in D. P. Ray, ed., *The Political Economy of Contemporary Africa* (1959).
5. For an illustration, see Aristide R. Zolberg, *One-Party Government in the Ivory Coast* (1964), chap. X.
6. Merle Kling, "Toward a Theory of Power and Political Instability in Latin America," *Western Political Quarterly*, IX, 1 (March 1956), 33–34.
7. "The Congo," in Gwendolen M. Carter, ed., *Five African States* (1963).

8. In an interview with Francis Monheim, *La Metropole* (Antwerp: April 1, 1964).

9. William Cutteridge, *Armed Forces in New States* (1963), pp. 51–52.

10. *Le Soir* (Brussels: March 25, 1964).

11. *La Libre Belgique* (Brussels: March 13, 1964).

12. Army pay was increased 450 per cent during the first year of independence.

13. Edward Shils, "The Military in the Political Development of the New States," in John J. Johnson, ed., *The Role of the Military in Underdeveloped Countries* (1962), p. 33.

14. David C. Rapoport, *Praetorianism: Government Without Authority* (forthcoming).

15. David C. Rapoport, "A Comparative Theory of Military and Political Types," in Samuel P. Huntington, ed., *Changing Patterns of Military Politics* (1962), pp. 73–74.

16. Mainly from the United States, Belgium, Israel, and Italy. U.S. military aid for the fiscal year 1963 was $3,378,000. Assistant Secretary of State W. Averell Harriman recently pledged continuation of U.S. military aid to the Congo for an undetermined period of time.

17. Edward Shils, *op. cit.*, pp. 55, 58.

18. Raymond L. Buell, *The Native Problem in Africa*, Vol. 2 (1928), p. 466.

19. International Institute of Differing Civilizations, *Staff Problems in Tropical and Subtropical Countries* (1962), p. 174.

20. René Lemarchaud, "The Rise of Congolese Nationalisms," quoted in *Five African States* (1963), p. 107.

21. See Joseph S. Nye, Jr., "The Impact of Independence on Two African Nationalist Parties," mimeographed seminar paper (Boston University: 1964), p. 34 ff.

22. Notably at Kabare, near Bukavu. See *The New York Times* (October 23, 1963).

23. M. Crawford Young, "Congo Political Parties Revisited," *Africa Report* (January 1963), p. 20.

24. S. N. Eisenstadt, in J. La Palombara, ed., *Bureaucracy and Political Development* (1963), p. 110.

25. *Ibid.*, p. 112.

26. Fred W. Riggs, in J. La Polombara, ed., *Bureaucracy and Political Development* (1963), p. 126.

27. *Ibid.*, p. 129.

28. Loi no. 63/411 of May 17, 1963, *Journal Official* (June 6, 1963), pp. 325–327, and Decret no. 63/158 of June 8, 1963, *Journal Official* (July 1, 1963), p. 408.

29. An informal caucus that includes Army Chief Mobutu, Security Chief Nendaka, Justice (formerly Foreign) Minister Bomboko, and a number of high officials of the Defense and Interior ministries.

30. *Remarques Congolaises* (Brussels: December 29, 1963), no. 30 ff. This periodical was subsequently banned in the Congo. See also "Tshombe: right-left-left," *Africa 1964* (April 3, 1964).

31. *Afrique Nouvelle*, 867 (Dakar: March 20–26, 1964), 8.

32. ". . . You represent here the most complete spectrum of national opinion. Could we have found a better representation than that of the present assembly? Who shall validly contest (your) mandate? . . . Popular verdict alone shall decide." Excerpts from President Kasavubu's opening speech in Luluabourg, January 10, 1964, quoted in *Etudes Congolaises*, VI, 2 (February 1964), 28.

33. *Ibid.*, p. 29.

34. *Le Soir* (April 14, 1964).

35. *Ibid.*

36. Seymour Martin Lipset, *Political Man*, 2nd ed. (1963), p. 64.

37. Translated from *La guerra de guerrilla* (1960), p. 12.

2. *Political Influence in Southern Nigeria*

1. For background reading on Nigeria, James S. Coleman, *Nigeria: Background to Nationalism* (1958), should be regarded as a basic reference work. This may be supplemented by my *Power and Stability in Nigeria* (1962), K. W. J. Post, *The Nigerian Federal Election* (1963), and Richard Sklar, *Nigerian Political Parties* (1963). More recent developments are conveniently summarized in the biweekly *West Africa*. An excellent bibliographical source on Nigeria is James O'Connel's "A Survey of Selected Social Science Research on Nigeria Since the End of 1957," in Robert A. Tilman and Taylor Cole, eds., *The Nigerian Political Scene* (1962), Appendix. See also John Harris, *Books About Nigeria*, 4th ed. (1963).

2. Edward C. Banfield notes: "The advantage of studying government as patterns of influence is that attention is directed beyond the legal, formal arrangements by which things are 'supposed' to be done to the much more complicated ones by which they are 'really' done" (*Political Influence* [1961], p. 7). In some respects this has been one major concern of my previous study of Nigeria, *op. cit.* Hugh H. and Mabel Smythe, in their *The New Nigerian Elite* (1960), attempt to identify segments of the elite but base their findings largely on weak and unreliable sources.

3. Stated differently, influence here refers to social action primarily by a person upon a person, not a group. The basic concept is that developed by French and Raven in Dorwin Cartwright and Alvin Zander, eds., *Group Dynamics. Research and Theory* (1962), pp. 608–609. Their concept is restricted to "influence on the person, P, produced by a social agent, O, where O can be either another person, a role, a norm, a group, or part of a group." The focus of this research, then, is influence-wielding by social agents acting upon key political role-players in the political communication system with reference to authoritative decision-making on critical socio-economic issues.

4. These findings are based on my interpretation and evaluation of the raw interview data. This applies also to the description of the influence structure, to the prominence given to certain groups and practices, and to omissions. The groups selected here for discussion and analysis do not, of course, exhaust the list of groups cited by respondents. Analysis and evaluation were confined to those groups and segments which by the evidence available appeared to be endowed with sufficient influence potential to play significant roles in the decision-making processes.

5. Reinforced by a tightening of financial controls over local bodies by the regional Ministry of Local Government, Eastern Region, *Policy for Local Government* (Official Document No. 13 of 1963), p. 2.

6. On occasion, when deemed necessary, juju priests have been employed to impress voters with the consequences of voting for opposition candidates, hooligans were mobilized by individual politicians to stifle opposition in their constituencies, and employers were pressured to dismiss supporters of opposition groups in return for government contracts.

7. Respondents nearly always refer to tribalism as a "cultural" grouping, with "cultural" understood to be distinct from "political" interests and concerns.

8. Membership in these groups ranges from mere handfuls to thousands. In Enugu alone there were some 65 groups of this type registered in August 1963.

9. In Owerri, the local NCNC even organized a "welfare society" to lend greater effect to its own appeal for amenities addressed to the regional government.

10. In Port Harcourt, a group of intellectuals and professionals of reformist orientation organized a local welfare society primarily to oppose the local NCNC-dominated town council. The society was forced into political limbo in a short period of time.

11. Eastern Region, *Conference of Leading Citizens of Eastern Origin, 1960* (Enugu, 1960). This list of over 300 names was compiled in the Premier's office on advice of local government officials (provincial secretaries) who consulted their own informants to identify "the people who are most likely listened to." Personal interview with Permanent Secretary, Local Government, Eastern Region, July 1963.

12. The strike was successfully arbitrated for the government by one of the leading contractors in the Region (*West African Pilot* [August 14, 1963], p. 2). The chairman of the Eastern Working Committee of the NCNC, Dr. Mbanugo, asserted in the party press that the strike had been instigated by dissident "anti-party" elements.

13. Although the Mid-West Region was included in the survey, data related to it were not considered in this section.

14. Data collected also indicated stepped-up action by the Northern Region's Northern People's Congress (NPC) in the West and Mid-West, a development since amply confirmed.

15. The close tie-up between party-political considerations and public finance was revealed in the findings of the Coker Commission, Federation of Nigeria, *Report of the Coker Commission of Inquiry*, Vols. I–IV, Federal Ministry of Information, Lagos (1962). See also Federation of Nigeria, *Comments of the Federal Government on the Report of Coker Commission of Inquiry* . . . Federal Ministry of Information, Lagos (Sessional Paper No. 4 of 1962).

16. The attribution of *independent* power to traditional rulers on the part of observers of the contemporary political scene in

Nigeria appears not to be based on empirical data of any kind. In Abeokuta, the late Alake was alleged, by respondents, to have been instrumental in defeating a tax scheme backed by the regional government. On the other hand he may merely have perceived a strong current of public opposition, partly fanned by a political party, and, in the fashion of traditional rulers, identified himself surreptitiously with what he sensed to be the consensus of opinion.

17. Reference is made to the invocation of the prestige of the paramount ruler of Ibadan, the Olubadan, in behalf of a tax proposal. Traditional rulers, with few exceptions, seem to live in a dream world as far as their own concept of their influence potential is concerned.

18. In the combined Western and Mid-Western Regions, the Yorubas constituted a majority of approximately four-fifths of the total population.

19. My attention was drawn to the possibility that similar social and professional groups within different ethnic clusters may warrant different ratings with regard to their relative influence status and capabilities.

20. For example, the Western Nigeria Farmers' Council, ostensibly an independent interest group, turns out to be in fact an instrument of the ruling UPP, directly supervised by the Premier of the Western Region. It is a link in the communication chain leading from the top down instead of from the lower levels up. The rival All Nigeria Farmers' Congress appears to be in effect the creature and responsibility of the UPP's coalition partner, the NCNC.

21. Because the public in general, and most leaders as well, fail to understand or appreciate jurisdictional dividing lines, it is likely that the generalization can be made that anybody with a modicum of determination can and does see anybody about anything at any time. If this is so, caution would be in order in any tracing of lines of influence within a given administrative or political sector or sphere.

22. It may well be that members of this group exercise some long-range influence over those segments of the public who are competent to understand and inclined to appreciate their thoughts and ideas.

23. It has been brought to my attention that the leading daily newspapers, the *West African Pilot* and the *Daily Express,* appear

to be quite independent and to reflect the existence of factions in the ruling political parties. That there are factions in the ruling parties is of course not denied. The data gathered in the present survey appear, however, to indicate the relative impotence of these factions when it comes to the exercise of significant influence on decision-makers with regard to critical socio-economic issues. It is doubtful whether in the present setting factions can be identified sufficiently to be of value in a study of this kind. At any rate, some of the disagreements reflected in the press appear to be reflections of relatively ephemeral personality conflicts raging around the North-South and East-West discords rather than of deep-seated factional struggles which can be typed and classified meaningfully and systematically.

24. Bretton, *op. cit.*, p. 72 ff.

25. Frederik Harbison states: "In Nigeria, economic development is primarily a political rather than an economic question," in Robert Tilman and Taylor Cole, eds., *The Nigerian Political Scene* (1962), p. 219.

A random examination of the *West African Pilot* or the *Daily Express* between June 1 and September 1, 1963 provides evidence of the explosion of demands for amenities which has been under way for some time but has gained additional momentum with independence.

3. *Mass Party Regimes in Africa*

1. This paper was prepared with the aid of a 1963 Rockefeller Summer Research Grant.

2. See Crane Brinton, *The Jacobins* (1961).

3. For an excellent analysis of the social bases of the Wafd and the resulting internal strains, see Francis Bertier, "Les forces sociales à l'oeuvre dans le nationalisme égyptien," *Orient*, V (1958), 73–85.

4. For elaborations of this distinction, see Ruth Schachter, "Single Party Systems in West Africa," *American Political Science Review* (June 1961), pp. 294–307; and Thomas Hodgkin, *African Political Parties* (1961), pp. 68–75. Both authors express their indebtedness to Maurice Duverger's typology of Western political parties in *Political Parties* (1954), Part I.

5. See Sigmund Neumann, ed., *Modern Political Parties* (1956), pp. 404–405.

6. See Aristide R. Zolberg, *One-Party Government in the Ivory Coast* (1964), esp. pp. 142–144, 295–296, 319–320, for a discussion of the ethnically based local organization of the PDCI and its "dysfunctional" consequences for national integration.

7. See Carl J. Friedrich and Z. K. Brzezinski, *Totalitarian Dictatorship and Autocracy* (1956), pp. 9–10.

8. For a concise and amusing account of Sékou Touré's favorite expressions, see B. Charles, "Un parti politique africain: Le Parti Démocratique de Guinée," *Revue française de science politique* (June 1962), pp. 320–321.

9. Note Martin Kilson's astute observations about what may be "a unique feature of African politics," an economy in the use of repressive measures that Machiavelli so persuasively advocated; in "Authoritarian and Single-Party Tendencies in African Politics," *World Politics* (January 1963), p. 294.

10. R. C. Tucker, "Toward a Comparative Politics of Movement-Regimes," *American Political Science Review* (June 1961), pp. 281–289.

11. In Tunisia, for example, "Islamic Socialism" might provide a doctrinal basis, but it has yet to be fully elaborated apart from the passing references to Islam that Bourguiba has made in connection with "Neo-Destour Socialism." In Mali, Modibo Keita enunciated the beginnings of an Islamic Socialist doctrine ten years ago when he said: "The RDA, *L'Union Soudanaise,* is a second religion, the source of which is to be found in the Muslim religion that advocates aiding the poor and defending the weak" *Essor* (September 15, 1954), quoted by Thomas Hodgkin and Ruth S. Morgenthau in their very interesting essay on Mali in J. S. Coleman and Carl G. Rosberg, eds., *Political Parties and National Integration in Tropical Africa* (1964).

12. Political instability, of course, is quite possible outside the context of a revolutionary situation. The latter at least presupposes an important social sector alienated from the political order. In Africa the Marxist scheme need not apply; "economic development" is more apt to create an overabundance of students and disgruntled schoolteachers and government clerks than a revolutionary proletariat.

13. The term "dominant one-party system," as contrasted to the

above "mass party regime," should be reserved for cases in
which the opposition may matter, as in India. In the African
single-party context, opposition parties may serve to advertise
the regime's democratic character but are banned and de-
capitated if the regime feels threatened or too severely criticized. Thus, though it had nothing to do with the plot on
Bourguiba's life (December 24, 1962), the Tunisian Communist Party was outlawed and its official and unofficial
monthly newspapers banned. One may perhaps also be
skeptical of the difference between a *parti unique* and a *parti
unifié*. The latter, in Guinea and Mali, were the product of
party mergers which were supposedly voluntary. This explanation was given by Madeira Keita, a Mali politician, in "Le
Parti unique en Afrique," *Présence Africaine*, No. 30
(February–March 1960); the relevant excerpts are available
in English in Paul E. Sigmund, Jr., ed., *The Ideologies of the
Developing Nations* (1963), pp. 175–176. One may wonder
whether the minority party leaders really had any effective
political alternative; more to the point, do the internal
workings of the *parti unifié* after the merger allow for the
crystallization of *tendances* or factions and the competition
for power of alternative groups of leaders? The case of Mali
suggests a negative answer. After the riots of July 20, 1962, the
two top leaders of the (socialist) minority party that had
merged three years earlier were arrested and brought to trial.
One of them, Fily Dabo Sissoko, was made to confess his guilt:
"I was born to govern . . . I am feudal. . . ." But the
"People's Court" which sentenced them did not convincingly
demonstrate their connections with the instigators of the riots.
For a vivid account, see Victor D. Du Bois, "Mali Five Years
after the Referendum," *American Universities Field Service
Report*, West African series (May 1963).

14. Methodologically, it seems more honest to make those values
explicit which I believe are shared by most of the actors
concerned, than to hide them in functionalist analysis. It is
perhaps true that a one-party regime that does not perform
the tasks outlined on p. 92 will not long survive, but the con-
verse may be equally true. Functionalist analysis—presupposing
that there are certain functions an organism must perform to
survive—may be highly misleading in the fluid African context.

15. By a "political animal" I mean anyone sufficiently politicized

to require a political outlet for self-expression, opportunities to exercise influence, and channels (apart from the sham of universal suffrage) for selecting leaders. Different kinds of political animals may have different political horizons. Thus the peasant villager may be primarily concerned with selecting his own village leaders, whereas the student may feel a need to participate meaningfully in national politics.

16. See Lucian W. Pye, *Politics, Personality, and Nation Building: Burma's Search for Identity* (1962), p. 39.

17. Note H. A. R. Gibb's observation about the Middle East: "It is precisely the great weakness of Arab countries that, since the breakdown of the old corporations, no social institutions have evolved through which the public will can be canalized, interpreted, defined and mobilized. . . . There is . . . no functioning organ of social democracy at all." Quoted from W. Z. Lacqueur, ed., *The Middle East in Transition* (1958), p. 8. One aspect of the problem he raises is that the societies in question lack any local organs of integration.

18. I would agree with Martin Kilson, "Authoritarian and Single-Party Tendencies in African Politics," *World Politics* (January 1963), that their democratic character is not the only significant yardstick for appraising mass party regimes. Recruitment, education, and integration provide other standards. All four of my criteria, however, are closely interrelated. I would tend to disagree with Lucy Mair's comment, which Kilson approvingly quotes (p. 293): "The crucial problem for the new governments seems likely to be how to be authoritarian enough to maintain stability and carry through their modernizing policies, and yet not so obviously oppressive as to provoke active or passive resistance." Without some measure of meaningful (democratic), as contrasted to ritual participation, many of the modernizing policies are apt to be failures—if one accepts the assumption that modernization involves changes of values and motivations as well as economic indices.

19. John Kautsky, in his *Political Change in Underdeveloped Countries* (1962), esp. pp. 106–107, 116–117, seems to be suggesting that as these mass party regimes succeed in developing their countries, they will automatically be transformed into democracies unless their intellectuals impose totalitarian rule. The assumption is that as a society modernizes, it becomes more highly differentiated. The new interests are either more

or less satisfied bargaining within the political system (then it is "democracy") or they are repressed ("totalitarianism"). My main objection to this view is that it considerably over-simplifies political reality while omitting discussion of the crucial problem: What is the political structure to be, in which interests (and ideas and personalities) express them-selves, cooperate, and compete? I. Wallerstein, in *Africa: The Politics of Independence* (1961), pp. 163–164, 166, also sug-gests that, as modernization pursues its course, the various auxiliary organizations of the mass party *may* acquire more influence. But their effective participation in the political process would seem easier to engineer now, when they are relatively weak, than later, when they could be more of a threat to the powers that be.

20. Ruth Schachter asserts restricted suffrage to be really "a greater threat to democracy than the existence of but a single party" (p. 305). The statement is a tautology if by democracy is meant formal mass participation. But, if participation is to be meaningful, that is, influence policy or the selection of leaders, the statement is highly questionable. Actually, as Kilson points out (p. 293), Schachter's definition of democracy is inadequate because it does not include the right to organize, as well as to express opposition.

21. In Guinea, there is only one national constituency (but though the Political Bureau as of 1963 nominates one-fifth of the slate, the rest are named by the party's regional federations). Some of the other mass party regimes go to less extreme lengths with multi-member constituencies and coincidentally accord a slightly more important role to the parliament. However, the centralized party remains the mediator between deputies and their constituents.

22. In "The National Party: A Tentative Model," *Public Policy*, X (1960), 262, I suggested that the auxiliaries might achieve greater autonomy after independence—thus paving the way for a stabilized competition based on interest within the party complex. But subsequent trends in all the mass party regimes have been just the reverse! Not untypical was the take-over of the trade union movement in Ghana by a man who had the encouragement of Nkrumah and the CPP (Convention People's Party) but very little labor support; in 1961, the Sekondi-Takoradi strikes were directed as much against the official

trade union as against the government. On balance, however, the fact that mass party regimes encourage the development of auxiliary organizations, even though under strict tutelage from above, probably has the effect of making the political process more elastic than it might otherwise be. For these regimes (not unlike the French *ancien régime*, though for different reasons) put themselves in the position of having to make concessions to special interests in order to stimulate the desired political participation.

23. For a specific illustration of the bargaining process between interests as it affected a specific decision, see C. A. Micaud, L. C. Brown, C. H. Moore, *Tunisia: The Politics of Modernization* (1964), pp. 105–107. As for the selection of national leaders, the auxiliary organizations of most mass party regimes are consulted by the party in drawing up electoral lists for parliament (though the locus of decision-making lies elsewhere).

24. By "dialectic" I mean a process of intellectual interaction between opposing ideas and values which serves to articulate the differences and also to provide a common framework of discourse for resolving or at least clarifying them. Socrates was the first to practice this method. By "dialectic" I do not mean to invoke a doctrine of historic determinism but rather to suggest a cultural, psychological, and political schema for explaining the development of a modernizing elite as the result of a series of interactions between colonizer and colonized elite in intensive colonial situations. Without accepting Hegel's dialectical "logic," I found his discussion of the relationship between master and slave illuminating in C. J. Friedrich, ed., *Phenomenology of the Spirit* (1953), pp. 399–410. Also useful is Georges Balandier's concept of the colonial situation, in *Sociologie Actuelle de l'Afrique Noire*, rev. ed. (1963), pp. 3–38. He views it as an irreducible totality—the central phenomenon being colonial domination rather than property relations or some other attribute (Marx would treat alienation in the more limited context of man's relationship to the means of production). For some of the psychological dimensions of alienation in the colonial setting, see O. Mannoni, *Prospero and Caliban* (1956). An interesting sociological analysis that stems from the author's African experiences and tries to reconcile the dialectical with the functional approach is to be found in P. L. van den Berghe, "Dialectic and Functionalism: Toward a

Theoretical Analysis," *American Sociological Review* (October 1963), pp. 675–705.

25. Max Weber's concept of charisma is beset with an extra-ordinary amount of ambiguity, as Carl J. Friedrich has shown in his article, "Political Leadership and the Problem of the Charismatic Power," *Journal of Politics*, XXIII (1961), 3–24. For the connection between charisma and legitimacy, see also his book, *Man and His Government* (1963), pp. 235–236. Yet, though Friedrich *contra* Weber would restrict charisma to apply to what the religious believer would consider to be a gift of God, there is an attenuated nonreligious usage of "charisma" that is of help to political sociologists, especially in under-developed countries. A leader *or a party* may enjoy among the followers a certain prestige and mystical aura derived from spectacular successes. The *mystique*, or "charisma," is fragile and certainly not a sufficient condition for legitimacy, which requires some shared values. Under favorable conditions, however, the party may retain its mystique even after the leader has departed, especially if failures can be blamed on individuals rather than on the party. Thus, apart from its particular activi-ties, the party may continue to serve as an integrating symbol for the new nation. Though this line of analysis seems more applicable to Guinea, Mali, or Tunisia, it is discussed by W. G. Runciman in his stimulating article, "Charismatic Legiti-macy and One-Party Rule in Ghana," *Archives européennes de sociologie*, IV (1963), 148–165, esp. 159 ff.

26. Tunisia provides the historical data suggesting this frame of analysis. See C. A. Micaud *et al.*, *op. cit.*, pp. 3–66, 73–88.

27. B. Charles, *op. cit.* In 1962 only 47 of the original 70 elected deputies were still deputies, the others having been appointed to administrative positions. The regime did not consider the National Assembly sufficiently important to organize by-elec-tions. The assembly could meet for a maximum of two sessions of two months each per year. Often legislation was taken by ordinance or decree, of which the assembly was simply in-formed.

28. Note Touré's talk about people of professional training being "depersonalized by the universal truths" they learned abroad. See L. Gray Cowan, "Guinea," in Gwendolen M. Carter, ed., *African One-Party States* (1962), p. 196.

29. It is perhaps not an accident that the countries tending to adopt the neo-Leninist model were former French territories—

where the colonial power had not fostered an indigenous civil
service tradition—rather than ex-British territories like Ghana,
which had one. Probably, too, differences in the metropolitan
political cultures had an impact, as did simple differences in
timing—postwar Paris being more conducive to neo-Leninist
ideas than the prewar environment which marked the Tunisian
neo-Destour leadership.

30. He is virtually the sole articulator of party ideology. With a
handful of close associates he controls the Political Bureau,
just as Bourguiba controls his. As chief of state he is elected
by universal suffrage to a seven-year term (Bourguiba's is only
five, coincident with the National Assembly), and his ministers
are responsible only to him. His comment that he is "responsible" to the National Assembly (elected for a five-year
term) may be dismissed as rhetoric. The one case of genuine
collective leadership, where the Political Bureau actually does
make all the crucial policy decisions, appears to be in Mali—
possibly because the party's founder-leader died before independence. In the words of Du Bois, *op. cit.*, whereas inner-
core leaders of the PDG's Political Bureau are "a law unto
themselves," the nineteen-man Political Bureau of the Union
Soudanaise is "a much more collegial body, responsive and
accountable to the larger ethnic and regional groups which its
various members represent and in whose name they speak."

31. With Mohammed Khider's resignation as general secretary of
the party in April 1963, the prospect of a reorganized FLN
dominating the government was eliminated. The long awaited
FLN congress, held in the spring of 1964, confirmed Ben
Bella's leadership.

32. Bourguiba, for instance, has great ability to project his ex-
ceptionally forceful personality and to articulate new values.
But he is "charismatic" only in the attenuated sense discussed
above (n. 25); the use of this term ought not to obscure the
fact that to his people he cannot escape the reputation of being
an atheist—and his religious reforms have encountered resistance.

33. R. Schachter, *op. cit.*, p. 296. Schachter also claims that Touré
and Keita "enjoyed a type of charisma which was limited both
by the constitutional procedures they themselves insisted upon
within their mass parties, and by the power exercised to a
greater or lesser extent by other groups and individuals within
the party."

34. Dr. Schachter had previously placed Togo's CUT (Comité de l'Unité Française) as one of the least effective parties in her mass party category. When Olympio was assassinated, the party seemed helpless in face of only a few hundred renegade soldiers.

35. For an example of a relatively democratic political process at the local level, see my "Politics in a Tunisian Village," *Middle East Journal* (Late Autumn 1963), pp. 527–540.

36. Recruitment can, of course, be better measured for parties where membership is not quasi-obligatory. Thus, in the more politically sophisticated regions of Tunisia, such as the Sahel, membership dropped in half five years after independence (though admittedly membership increased in more backward areas). But an equally meaningful sign of recruitment, in the sense of interested participation by political animals, is the negative index of grumbling, apathy, or discontent among the more articulate sectors—students, teachers, low-grade civil servants. Wildcat strikes are another index. In Muslim societies the attitudes of religious leaders—what they say in the mosque—may also be important.

37. Interestingly, the PDG of Guinea cleverly minimizes deliberation by arranging regional congresses only *after* the national congress has laid down the party line.

38. The Tunisian neo-Destour's National Council might have provided a useful deliberative forum. It was supposed to meet every six months but met only after independence until March 1962. Then it was convened to circumvent the calling of the scheduled national congress (the problem of Bizerte had not been solved); again in March 1963, it was called to reorganize the party structure.

4. *African Politics in the United Nations*

1. UN Doc. A/PV. 1220 (September 30, 1963).
2. UN Doc. A/PV. 1231 (October 7, 1963).
3. UN Doc. A/PV. 1238 (October 11, 1963).
4. UN Doc. A/PV. 1238 (October 11, 1963).
5. UN Doc. A/PV. 1216 (September 25, 1963).
6. In United Nations phraseology the term "geographical distribution" is generally used instead of its true meaning, "political balance."

7. UN Doc. A/PV. 1221 (September 30, 1963).

8. From the statement of Mr. Wachuku of Nigeria in UN Doc. A/PV. 1221 (September 30, 1963).

9. In *Africa in the United Nations* (1963).

5. *The Primacy of Political Development*

1. See, e.g., Seymour Martin Lipset, *Political Man: The Social Bases of Politics* (1960), pp. 27–63; Daniel Lerner, *The Passing of Traditional Society: Modernizing the Middle East* (1958), pp. 43–75; Karl W. Deutsch, "Social Mobilization and Political Development," *American Political Science Review*, LV (September 1961), 493–514.

2. Gabriel A. Almond, in Gabriel A. Almond and James S. Coleman, eds., *The Politics of the Developing Areas* (1960), p. 6.

3. James S. Coleman, *ibid.*, p. 576. Italics supplied.

4. See Herbert J. Spiro, "Comparative Politics: A Comprehensive Approach," *American Political Science Review*, LVI (September 1962), 577–595.

5. Almond, *op. cit.*, p. 17, and *passim*.

6. Seymour Martin Lipset, *The First New Nation: The United States in Historical and Comparative Perspective* (1963).

7. See Herbert J. Spiro, "New Political Forms in Africa," *World Politics*, XIII (October 1960), 69–76.

8. For a critique of the concept, see Herbert J. Spiro, "Totalitarianism," *International Encyclopedia of the Social Sciences* (forthcoming).

Appendix

1. For additional comments on interview techniques in Africa, see the note on that subject in Bretton, *op. cit.*, pp. 183–188.

2. Lucian W. Pye, "The Non-Western Political Process," *Journal of Politics*, XX, 3 (August 1958), 470.

3. Dorwin Cartwright and Alvin Zander, eds., *Group Dynamics, Research and Theory* (1962), pp. 609–610, n. 2.

4. In the absence of adequate telephone books and street directories, investigators are advised to obtain more than one point

of reference for the location of addresses, for this information also is likely to be grossly misleading.

5. A typical response was that obtained in Ibadan, where the local paramount chief was nominated consistently. When pressed for substantiating evidence, the response was: "After all, he *is* the Olubadan," or similar expressions.

INDEX

Studies in Political Science